EX LIBRIS

CASSELL'S DIRECTORY OF

Scented Plants

CASSELL'S DIRECTORY OF

Scented Plants

EVERYTHING YOU NEED TO CREATE A GARDEN

DAVID SQUIRE

Consultant Editor
LUCY HUNTINGTON

CASSELL&CO

Distributed in the United States of America
by Sterling Publishing Co., Inc.
387 Park Avenue South, New York, NY 10016-8810

A CIP Catalogue record for this book is
available from the British Library

ISBN 0 304 35601 8

This book was conceived, designed, and produced by
THE IVY PRESS LIMITED
The Old Candlemakers, West Street,
Lewes, East Sussex BN7 2NZ

Creative Director: PETER BRIDGEWATER
Designers: AXIS DESIGN
Editorial Director: DENNY HEMMING
Managing Editor: ANNE TOWNLEY
Illustrations: VANESSA LUFF & PETER BULL
Picture Researcher: LIZ EDDISON

Originated and printed by Hong Kong Graphic, Hong Kong

This book is typeset in Linotype Perpetua and Univers

CASSELL & CO
Wellington House, 125 Strand
London WC2R 0BB

ACKNOWLEDGMENTS

t *top* **b** *below* **l** *left* **r** *right* **Directory** *a–f, starting from top*

Liz Eddison 2, 5, 12tr, 14tr, 16tr, 17, 18bl,tr, 33l, 37l,r, 51, 95f /
Designer: Fiona Lawrenson 4 / Designer: Georgina Steeds 34r
The Garden Picture Library / Philippe Bonduel 80c / Densey
Clyne 10–11 / Eric Crichton 34l, 36l, 47 / Geff Dann 102b /
Sunnvia Harte 35l / Neil Holmes 32l / Stephen Jury 80a / Marie
O'Hara 14b, 15 / Jerry Pavia 103b / Howard Rice 84f, 88e, 93c /
Gary Rogers 30–31 / David Russell 80d / JS Sira 16bl, 38, 48 /
Friedrich Strauss 53
John Glover 6, 7, 12bl, 13, 19, 20 & 56–57, 22, 26, 28, 32r,
33r,36r, 54, 112 / Designer: Dan Pearson 35r
Lucy Huntington 80f
Peter McHoy 24 & 72t, 60a,f, 61a,b,e, 62a,d, 63c,e,f, 64e, 65f,
66c,e,f, 67a,f, 68a,e, 69a, 70c,d, 71a,b,e,f, 72a,c, 73c,d,e, 74b,
75b,f, 76a,c,d, 77b,e, 78b, 79a,c,f, 81f, 82b,d,e,f, 83b, 84a,b,c,e,
85b,c,d,e, 86d,e, 87b,c,d,e,f, 88b,c, 89c, 90b,c,d,f, 91b, 92b,d,f,
93a,b,d,e, 94b,f, 95a,c,e, 96a,c,d,e, 97a,b,c,d,e,f, 98a,b,c,e,f,
99c, 100a,c,f, 101a,b,c,d,f, 102d,f, 103c,e,f, 104d, 105a,e,f,
106c,d, 107a,d,f
The Harry Smith Collection 60b,c,e, 61d,f, 62b,e, 63a,b,d,
64b,c,d, 65a,b,c,d,e, 66a,b,d, 67b,d,e, 68b,c,d, 69b,d,f, 70a,b,e,f,
71c,d, 72c,d,e,f, 73a,b,f, 74a,f, 75a,c, 76b,f, 77a,d,f, 78a,c,d,e,f,
79b,d,e, 80b,e, 81a,b,c,d,e, 82a,c, 83a,e, 85a,f, 86f, 88d, 89a,b,
91a,d,e, 92a, 94a,c,d,e, 95b,d, 96f, 99b,d,e,f, 100b,e, 102a, 103a,
104a,b,e,f, 105b,c,d, 106a,b,e,f, 107b, c,e
David Squire 60d, 61c, 62c,f, 64a,f, 67c, 68f, 69c,e, 74c,d,e,
75e,f, 76e, 77c, 83c,d,f, 84d, 86a,b,c, 87a, 88a,f, 89d,e.f, 90a,e,
91c,f, 92c,e, 93f, 96b, 98d, 99a, 100d, 101e, 102c,e, 103d, 104c

CONTENTS

INTRODUCTION

Gardens that are rich in fragrant plants have qualities that are not normally revealed by those gardens which are unscented. They are, of course, richly bathed in exciting fragrances, but they have a further quality that is generated specifically by fragrance—they are friendly and reveal a lively ambience. Few people, once they have detected an unusual and captivating scent in a garden, can resist tracing it to its source, and smelling a perfumed flower will often lead them to smell leaves and stems too. Once the plant has been detected, there is usually a call to other gardeners to "come and smell this."

Scented plants have enthralled gardeners for thousands of years. More than 2,000 years ago the Greek philosopher, writer, and botanist Theophrastus wrote about fragrant plants and perfumes, and other Greek writers followed suit. During the mid-1600s, John Evelyn, an English garden designer and writer, wrote of creating vast areas of scented plants that would cleanse the air. He recommended the use of lilac, roses, and, above all, rosemary. At that time in Spain it was said that the distinctive

THEN AND NOW

🐝 In the sixteenth century, according to Matthias de l'Obel, a French doctor and botanist, clary was added to ales to make them more heady and easier to drink. In more recent times, clary oil has been used as an aphrodisiac.

🐝 During earlier centuries, honey was the only source of sweetness for most people and therefore was highly prized. Balm is a favorite plant for bees and was used to wipe skeps and hives to keep the bees contented. More recently, it has been used to make a cooling tea for feverish patients.

LEFT *A carpet of pinks brings not only a splash of color but also a wonderful clovelike aroma to a garden border.*

fragrance of rosemary could be detected some 30 leagues off the coast. This was quite a claim, as a league is about 3 miles (5km)! Evelyn also suggested the planting of gilliflowers, cowslips, lilies, thyme, and marjoram.

Later that century, the English statesman and keen gardener Sir William Temple advocated the medicinal use of scent, saying, "Fumigation or the use of scent is not practiced in modern physic, but might be carried out with advantage, seeing that some smells are so depressing, or poisonous, and others so inspiriting and reviving." Additionally, he claimed that when walking through the Indian House in Amsterdam, where cloves, nutmegs, mace, and other spices were kept, he felt revived and exalted in health and humor. Many fragrant herbs, as well as spices from the East, were sold by street vendors, their names often interwoven in popular songs and street cries. Nowadays, many herbs still have medicinal uses. Lavender, for example, is used in aromatherapy to alleviate the symptoms of asthma and bronchitis.

RICH IN WILDLIFE

Whether in borders, trellises, or in garden ponds, plants rich in scent attract a wide range of insects, which in turn bring further interest and vitality to gardens. Butterflies and bees are especially attracted to sweet-smelling flowers during the day, while moths mainly appear at night. Flowers that have a fruity fragrance are often pollinated by beetles, whereas plants with a fetid nature, such as the yellow skunk cabbage (*Lysichiton americanus*), attract flies.

SCENTED PLANTS FOR ALL GARDENS

Within this book the aim has been to create a parade of fragrant plants for all parts of the garden, from borders packed with summer-flowering annuals to rose beds and arches. There are also trees and shrubs with fragrant flowers, and conifers with richly aromatic foliage.

Most of the plants featured in this book are described in the directory section, which gives details of their expected height and spread, the season when they create their display, and the type of fragrance they produce.

There is also detailed information on using and caring for scented plants, from buying and propagating them to creating specific areas of scent. These range from fragrant herb gardens and scented water gardens to terraces and patios enriched with scented plants in containers. Additionally, advice is offered on creating gardens rich in scent during all the seasons of the year.

This is a book on scented gardens that will enthrall you with the wide range of fragrances that can be created in your garden, from fruity aromas of raspberries and bananas to the penetrating richness of vanilla and chocolate.

ABOVE *Scented gardens can be practical as well as beautiful, introducing a range of aromatic seasonings into the kitchen.*

HOW TO USE THIS BOOK

Cassell's Garden Directories have been conceived and written to appeal both to gardening beginners and to confident gardeners who need advice for a specific project. Each book focuses on a particular type of garden, drawing on the experience of an established expert. The emphasis is on a practical and down-to-earth approach that takes account of the space, time, and money that you have available. The ideas and techniques in these books will help you to produce an attractive and manageable garden that you will enjoy for years to come.

Cassell's Directory of Scented Plants takes as its starting point one of the most attractive aspects of gardening, the delicious fragrance of plants and flowers. The book is divided into three sections. The opening section, *Planning Your Garden*, introduces the subject of aromatic plants, looking at the different kinds of effects that can be achieved and the range of scented plants that is available. There are also four specific inspirational garden plans for producing scented gardens for different seasons, and a plan to help you create a delightful garden for evening fragrance.

Part Two of the book, *Creating Your Garden*, moves on to the nitty-gritty of selecting, buying, and planting appropriate shrubs, herbs, and flowers. This section opens with some advice on the range of different features that you can choose from. Different spaces and climatic conditions, for instance, will lend themselves to different kinds of plants. There is also advice on appropriate and imaginative containers that can be used to create a fragrant corner.

The remainder of Part Two is packed with practical information on basic techniques such as sowing, feeding and weeding plants, dividing congested clumps, and supporting and pruning plants. Moving on from this basic groundwork, this section then encourages you to put your skills to use with a series of specific projects, such as creating a scented rose garden or a herb garden. There are step-by-step illustrations throughout this section that show clearly and simply what you need to do to achieve the best results. Also included are handy hints and tips, points to watch out for, and star plants that are particularly suitable for the projects that are described.

The final part of the book, *The Plant Directory*, is a comprehensive listing of dozens of plants that will bring scent to your garden. Each plant is illustrated, and the accompanying text and symbol chart give complete information on appropriate growing conditions, speed of growth, and ease of maintenance.

GARDEN DESIGNS are included to inspire you to great things in your own garden.

COLOR PHOTOGRAPHS show what can be achieved with a little effort and imagination.

3D PLANS show the best planting plan for you to achieve the right effect.

THE KEY FEATURES of each plant used are described to help you visualize the plan.

CHOICES *show a selection of plants, garden furniture, or other features that might be appropriate in your garden.*

COLOR PHOTOGRAPHS *help you to decide on the appropriate feature for your garden.*

EXPLANATORY TEXT *describes the various possibilities available in each category.*

CLEAR ILLUSTRATIONS *show each step of the process.*

THE CHECKLIST *details important things to look out for in choosing garden features.*

PRACTICAL SUGGESTIONS *give useful information on basic techniques and garden projects.*

WATCHPOINTS BOXES *give a checklist of cautions and problems to look out for.*

THE PLANT DIRECTORY *is organized into categories, making it simple to find a particular type of plant.*

COLOR PHOTOGRAPHS *clearly identify each plant listed.*

CLEAR DESCRIPTIVE TEXT *details the appearance and the appropriate growing conditions for each plant.*

THE SYMBOLS PANEL *gives important information on features such as speed of growth and shade tolerance.*

SIDEBAR *shows at a glance the season of interest for each plant.*

PLANNING YOUR GARDEN

1

There are many distinctive types of scented garden features, from a rustic arbor festooned with scented roses to a fragrant hanging basket. This section surveys the options and helps you decide what will best fit your needs.

Covering the diverse selection of scents, it suggests ways in which you might like to use scent, from central features to aromatic vignettes. This section concludes with a series of garden plans that give you the option of year-round fragrance and interest.

LEFT *The beautiful climbing rose 'Zéphirine Drouhin' is fragrant and, unusually, thornless. Prune back hard if you want to grow it as a shrub.*

WHY AND HOW PLANTS ARE SCENTED

Scent has long played an important role in our lives. According to the anthropologist Dr. Louis Leakey, humans survived their early years on earth because their offensive body odor kept predators at bay. This unseen protective curtain is believed to have disappeared when humans learned to use weapons for defense. It is therefore not surprising that we still harbor a fascination with natural fragrances.

Most people are able to detect a wide range of smells, but we do not all have this ability to the same degree. Women generally have a keener sense of smell than men (though it is said that this diminishes during pregnancy), and there is also a theory that dark-haired people usually have a more sensitive appreciation of scents than those with fair hair.

Our sense of smell is claimed to be much more acute and perceptive than that of taste. This often depends on the nature of the smell. Unpleasant odors such as decaying meat can be detected at very low levels, and escaping gas can also be sensed at levels not discernible by gas-detecting equipment. By contrast, more refined scents such as violets are often detectable at first, but soon fail to make an impression. Later, however, a further inhalation will again reveal their bouquet. It is as if after being initially saturated with a delicate scent, the nose needs a rest before making a further appreciation.

THEN AND NOW

🍃 Many aromatic plants have a history of use for cleansing, including rue (*Ruta graveolens*), used as a strewing plant to prevent the spread of jail fever. It was also an essential ingredient of the famed "Vinegar of the Four Thieves," which was used by thieves in Marseilles to enter plague-infested houses with impunity.

🍃 Nowadays, its uses are less villainous and the leaves are used medicinally by herbalists to ease backache and joint pains.

SCENTED FLOWERS

The function of scent in flowers is usually to act as part of the reproductive mechanism. The range of insects that pollinate flowers includes bees, wasps, flies, butterflies, moths, and beetles. Occasionally, birds act as pollinators.

Butterflies are especially attracted by shrubs such as lavender, privet, lilac, and buddleja (buddleia), as well as herbaceous perennials like asters, and *Sedum spectabile*, the succulently leaved showy stonecrop. *Buddleja davidii* is so popular with these insects that it is commonly known as the butterfly bush. From midsummer through to mid-autumn it bears plumelike spires of lilac-purple flowers that are frequently festooned with butterflies.

Night-scented plants usually have a penetratingly sweet perfume to guide moths to white or blandly colored flowers. A strong scent is essential, as these flowers often have a short life and it is vital that insects find them before they fade and die. Additionally, scent tends to be more powerful at night, when the air is usually damper.

LEFT *Scented plants are an essential part of a wildlife garden, their aroma proving irresistible to a range of beautiful creatures from honey bees to butterflies.*

Flowers that attract beetles usually emit a fruity bouquet and are fully open. This is because, like flies, beetles have short tongues (unlike butterflies and moths which have long tongues). Flies delight in disgusting smells and therefore pollinate plants that do not appeal to other insects, such as the strikingly colored yellow skunk cabbage (*Lysichiton americanus*) and stinking Benjamin (*Trillium erectum*), both from North America. Other "stinkers" beloved by flies are lords-and-ladies (*Arum maculatum*), which have a urinous stench, stinking hellebore (*Helleborus foetidus*), and fetid bugbane (*Cimicifuga foetida*), both with a putrid smell.

POINTS TO CONSIDER

❧ Many culinary herbs develop seeds used to flavor food. These are best grown in a warm, wind-protected position in a garden, enabling seed heads and pods to ripen.
❧ Small herbs grown for their leaves can be planted in large pots on a patio, or in a windowbox or trough.

SCENTED LEAVES

Oily vapors in leaves serve several vital functions: they keep plants cool by creating a barrier between the warmth of the sun and their surfaces, and reduce the loss of moisture from plants. Indeed, many of the fragrant-leaved plants that we grow in our gardens are native to warm, dry regions. Experiments in the twentieth century confirm the cooling ability of scented leaves. Rosemary, thyme, and lavender in particular have this quality.

In addition, the vapor created by scented-leaved plants often repels insects; in creating protection from animals, the scent can assume the role of thorns. Scented-leaved pelargoniums (geraniums) combine such a protective scent with hairy leaves to put up an almost impregnable defense against potential pests. Some scents have an antiseptic value: the bark of a few trees and conifers such as balsam popular (*Populus balsamifera*) and balsam fir (*Abies balsamea*) exude a gum with this quality.

ABOVE *The skunk cabbage (Lysichiton americanus) has a fetid aroma that is appealing to many insects. The yellow spathes that are produced in spring are real showstoppers.*

TYPES OF SCENT IN FLOWERS

Flowering plants are the main source of scent in gardens, combining fragrance with color and attractive shapes. The ones suggested here have unusual fragrances grouped under the general headings of fruity, floral, sweet, and savory. Flowers have an ephemeral nature, some appearing for only a day, but whatever their lifespan, there is a wide range of plants that create color and scent throughout the year. Fragrant winter gardens are a special delight, and a medley of scented shrubs and bulbs helps to bridge late autumn and early spring.

The rambling rose *Rosa* 'François Juranville', the Modern Shrub rose *R.* 'Nymphenburg', and the rambling rose *R.* 'René André' all produce flowers with an applelike scent in summer. The deciduous shrub *Genista hispanica* takes this scent and mingles it with pineapple, while the deciduous tree *Calycanthus floridus* (Carolina allspice) adds a hint of strawberry to the apples.

If you desire a slightly sharper aroma, choose *R.* 'Cerise Bouquet', which creates a raspberry fragrance. *Rosa* 'Veilchenblau' bears flowers with an orange scent, while *Magnolia sieboldii, R.* 'Heritage', and *R.* 'Madame Hardy' possess a delightful zesty lemon aroma. The evergreen

shrub *Coronilla valentina glauca* and *Iris graminea* (beardless iris) emit a wonderful plumlike scent, while *Cytisus battandieri* (Moroccan broom) produces an altogether more tropical scent in late spring and early summer—a wonderful pineapple fragrance.

FLORAL SCENTS

Some plants produce a fragrance that is reminiscent of a radically different species. *Gladiolus tristis concolor* (evening flower gladiolus) gives off a carnationlike fragrance, while *Hedysarum coronarium* (French honeysuckle) produces a rich, honeylike scent that is suggestive of clover. Other

RIGHT *The old rose* Rosa gallica 'Versicolor' *is the stunning centrepiece of a glorious summer border. Other cottage garden favourites—lavender, stock, and rosemary—add to the delicious fragrance.*

The vast range of distinctive fragrances in plants is a result of volatile oils in their flowers, leaves, stems, roots, and seeds. These volatile oils are also known as essential oils or attar, and earlier as otto, especially when applied to roses.

One way of extracting volatile oils is by distillation. Distillation involves placing plant material (usually flowers) in steam; the oils evaporate and mix with the steam. When the steam condenses the essential oil separates and floats on the surface. This is removed and further distilled to create an essence of greater purity.

Another way of extracting volatile oils is by *enfleurage*, which is said to be superior to distillation. *Enfleurage* involves placing the plant material on filters positioned in a bowl of oil. The oil slowly absorbs the volatile oils. As plants become depleted of oils they are replaced with fresh material; the process continues until the oil in the bowl is well saturated with volatile oils. Then the essence is extracted from the oil by distillation, and dissolved in vegetable oils.

plants with this character-istic are *Clematis rehderiana*, which smells of cowslips, and *Galanthus nivalis* (common snowdrop), which produces a distinctive and unusual mossy smell during the winter months.

ABOVE A small courtyard setting intensifies the fragrance of these roses, which jostle with petunias and French marigolds.

The scent of some plants is inimitable. Plant *Lavandula officinalis* (English lavender), a.k.a. *L. angustifolia*, or *Lavandula stoechas* (French lavender) for an unforgettable aromatic feast. To introduce the fragrance of lilac into your scented garden, plant the sweet-smelling *Syringa microphylla*.

The common snowdrop (*Galanthus nivalis*) has a delicate appearance that belies its hardiness. In earlier years, it was grown in monastery gardens on account of its association with purity and the Feast of the Purification of the Virgin in February, when it flowers.

Herbalists today claim that the roots when sliced and steeped in light beer produce a lotion that eases chilblains and frostbite.

SWEET SCENTS

Many plants produce wonderfully mellifluous aromas that steep a garden in sweetness and the smell of honey. *Buddleja globosa* (orange-ball tree), *Crocus chrysanthus, Iris danfordiae,* and *Ulex europaeus* all have this lingering and often heavy fragrance. For musklike smells, try the well-known shrub *Buddleja davidii* (butterfly bush), the hardy annual *Centaurea moschata* (sweet sultan), or *Rosa* 'Daybreak'. To introduce pastoral charm to an urban garden, sow the annual *Lobularia maritima* (sweet alyssum), which will fill the air with the bouquet of freshly mown hay.

SAVORY SMELLS

As a counterpoint to a plethora of sweet smells, nature has given us many species that emit a more savory aroma. For a clovelike fragrance, plant *Aquilegia vulgaris* (columbine), while for an almond scent choose the bulbous *Galanthus allenii* (snowdrop) or opt for *Chimonanthus praecox* for a spicy fragrance. Finally, to provide sustenance and relief from the tribulations of modern life, plant *Nuphar lutea* (brandy bottle), a water plant that gives off the warming aroma of brandy.

SCENT IN LEAVES, STEMS, SEEDS, AND BARK

*S*cents occur not solely in flowers but in all parts of plants, including leaves, roots, stems, fruits, seeds, and bark. They all combine to enrich gardens with a wide range of fragrances that bring a fresh quality to our lives throughout the year. Some, of course, can be taken indoors to create an atmosphere of freshness in our homes.

The range of fragrance in leaves is just as wide and exciting as in flowers—and the scents often last far longer. Fragrances occur in the leaves of many types of plants, from annuals and herbaceous perennials to scented-leaved pelargoniums (geraniums) and conifers. For example, clary (*Salvia sclarea*), a hardy biennial usually grown as an annual, has leaves that emit the fragrance of fresh grapefruit when bruised, while the oak-leaved geranium (*Pelargonium quercifolium*) has an almond scent with a hint of balsam. Conifers offer an impressive range of scents: the common juniper (*Juniperus communis*) has an applelike bouquet, while the pencil cedar (*Juniperus virginiana*) has the smell of paint with a hint of kitchen soap.

Mints are popular and can be grown in containers on patios. Apple mint (*Mentha suaveolens*) has leaves that emit the distinctive bouquet of apples. Ginger mint (*Mentha x gracilis*) is known for its spicy and ginger scent, with a tang of spearmint, while common mint (*Mentha spicata*) has a strong mint bouquet.

POINTS TO CONSIDER

❧ Mint is invasive, so plant it in containers on a patio. Alternatively, use bottomless buckets buried to their rims in garden soil; it helps to contain the plants' roots.

❧ Plant the biennial (sometimes short-lived perennial) angelica (*Angelica archangelica*) in herbaceous borders. Its aromatic leaves and large, umbrellalike flower heads create a distinctive feature. It is ideal for planting in a corner.

AROMATIC SEEDS

Many plants have seeds that can be used in cooking to give rich scents and flavors to food and drinks. Usually they are crushed to release their scent. Aniseed from the anise plant (*Pimpinella anisum*) has long been used to give a licorice flavor to cough mixtures, liquors, soups, cakes, and sweets. Caraway seeds (*Carum carvi*), with their distinctive and well-known aroma, are used to flavor bread, cakes, cheese, soups, and liquors, and also to perfume soap. Coriander (*Coriandrum sativum*) has seeds that give off an orangelike fragrance when dry. They are used to flavor pickles and curries, as well as being added to sugar in the making of sweets. Dill (*Anethum graveolens*) has seeds with a distinctively spicy bouquet that are added to cakes and bread, as well as to fish and rice dishes. Fennel (*Foeniculum vulgare*), like aniseed, produces seeds with the aromatic scent and flavor of licorice. They are often used when cooking oily fish such as mackerel.

LEFT *The beautiful reddish bark of the incense cedar* (Calocedrus decurrens) *forms large, coarse plates, which curl outward. When crushed, the bark gives off a very strong smell which is evocative of turpentine.*

FRAGRANT ROOTS

Several garden plants have fragrant roots, and although their scent is not readily detectable there is always a surprise awaiting when plants are lifted and divided. Blessed herb (*Geum urbanum*) is a herbaceous perennial with short, thick, rhizomatous roots that smell of cloves when dried. Chocolate root (*Geum rivale*), a moisture-loving plant that is ideal for planting in moist soil around a pond, has short, thick, rhizomatous roots that emit the bouquet of chocolate. Other plants with fragrant roots include licorice (*Glycyrrhiza glabra*) and sweet flag (*Acorus calamus*), which produces a camphorlike smell and was used in the past as a strewing herb in castles and churches.

FRAGRANT STEMS, GUMS, AND BARK

Anyone who has been in a lumber yard or cut wood at home will be aware of the soft and warm bouquet that wood reveals. There are also a few garden plants with fragrant stems, gums, and bark. Bog myrtle (*Myrica gale*) has wood and leaves that reveal a sweet and lemonlike fragrance when crushed. *Hebe cupressoides* has stems and leaves that emit the light bouquet of violets. For a balsamic scent, plant sweet gum (*Liquidambar styraciflua*), or for a bouquet of Russian leather with a hint of sweetness, opt for sweet birch (*Betula lenta*).

BELOW *Many herbs do not carry their fragrance in their flowers. Fennel is prized for the aniseed bouquet of its leaves.*

ADDING SCENT TO YOUR GARDEN

In a practical world, there is no such thing as a "perfect" site for scented plants. However, most gardeners are tenacious and not easily deterred from growing the plants they like, whatever the soil, aspect, or climate. Even if the conditions make garden-grown scented plants impossible, there are ways around the problem. Ephemeral scented plants can be grown in hanging baskets, troughs, and windowboxes, while tubs may be used for shrubs and slow-growing or miniature conifers.

The warmth of a south- or west-facing slope, perhaps cloistered from the rigors of cold wind, creates an ideal position for scented plants. These idyllic conditions help to prevent scents dispersing, as well as aiding plant growth.

In most gardens, this site has to be created: tall aromatic conifers can be used to reduce the wind's speed, while vigorous evergreens can be used to form a second barrier.

Within a garden, aromatic, low-growing hedges create attractive features alongside paths, and help break up a garden. A garden that can be seen in its totality at one glance soon loses its appeal, whereas one containing strategically placed trellises clothed in scented climbers, and screening hedges rich in fragrance, retains its appeal.

SEASONAL SCENTED GARDENS

We all have our favorite times of the year, and often these preferences are influenced by happenings during childhood or by birthdays. Scented plants for all four seasons are described on pages 20–27.

Gardens rich in fragrance during winter bring welcome winter cheer. Winter-fragrant shrubs and bulbs alongside a firm-surfaced path form an attractive feature, and while many winter-flowering shrubs are devoid of interest throughout the rest of the year, a few of the witch hazels have leaves that assume rich colors in autumn.

Spring is an anticipatory season and one that many gardeners ignore while awaiting the explosion of summer color. However, it is a season packed with scented shrubs and bulbs, which are featured on pages 20–21.

HINTS AND TIPS

🍂 Because damp, misty weather encourages scents to linger, plants that flower in early autumn, like *Buddleja davidii*, often have their fragrances strengthened.

🍂 Where fragrant, low-growing plants, such as some thymes, are planted in natural stone paths, do not use salt in winter to remove ice from the path's surface. Also, do not use a spade to clear snow.

LEFT *This rustic and informal path meanders through beds of lavender, with edgings of the attractively leaved* Helichrysum petiolare *which, toward the end of summer, bears curry-scented flowers. Fiery heads of kniphofia bring extra color to the display.*

Summer scent is prolific, particularly in border plants. Some of these fragrantly flowered or scented-leaved plants are so vigorous that they intrude over lawn edges and create bare areas. Installing a row of paving slabs along the edge both prevents this happening and helps to highlight the plants by reflecting light.

Autumn need not be scentless, and many fragrant plants that flower during this season are described on pages 24–25. Several shrubs and climbers carry their fragrance into this season, and some can be given a backdrop of shrubs and climbers with autumn-colored leaves.

FRAGRANT PATHS, LAWNS, AND SEATS

Although not a practical surface for continual use, especially when young children are around, a path formed of plants that emit a fragrance when their foliage is trodden upon is a delight. Several low-growing, aromatic plants can

be used, including thyme, which produces flowers in a range of colors, and chamomile. To decrease wear on the plants, use stepping stones in combination with the plants when constructing a scented path.

Grass seats have created unusual features for many years and are perfect for informal gardens. They are usually constructed on banks about 18in (45cm) high, where bricks or timbers constrain the soil. Instead of laying a strip of turf to form the seat, the soil can be planted with thyme or chamomile. Regular watering is essential to ensure that the plants become established quickly. If the scented bench is long, intersperse the plants with small paving slabs.

BELOW *An unspectacular piece of garden furniture has been transformed by the addition of a chamomile seat. Those who come over to this quiet corner of the garden will be rewarded with the perfect place to take a well-deserved rest.*

THE SCENTED SPRING GARDEN

*S*pring is the season of rebirth in gardens, with a wealth of fragrant flowers appearing
in increasing numbers. Many viburnums drench the air with penetratingly sweet
fragrances, while other shrubs such as daphnes, skimmias, and magnolias, as well as
the ever-popular lilac, tantalize the nose with a wide range of fragrances. Some of these
continue to flower into early summer but start their season in spring. For most, the precise
time of flowering depends on the prevailing local climate.

With the arrival of spring, there is a wonderful variety of
plants to mix and match with scented trees and shrubs.
Magnolia denudata (lily tree or yulan) is a slow-growing
magnolia that is ideal for a small garden until it is 15 or
20 years old. Its pure white, sweetly scented spring flowers
are eye-catching. Plant a sea of the blue-flowered *Muscari
armeniacum* (grape hyacinth) around it.

If you are a rose lover, then consider *Rosa* 'Helen
Knight', earlier known as *R. ecae* 'Helen Knight'. This is a
shrublike rose that develops fernlike foliage and lightly
scented, clear yellow, single flowers during May and into
June. Consider trailing plants like cytisus, and emphasize
its arching, tumbling nature by planting *Forsythia suspensa*,
with its yellow, pendulous flowers during March and early
April, behind it.

ABOVE *The evergreen shrub
Daphne odora 'Aureomarginata'
bears fragrant flowers from* *midwinter to early spring, and
its attractive variegated leaves
are a year-round pleasure.*

SPRING-FLOWERING BULBS

Spring is well known for its range of bulbs. The ubiqui-
tous daffodils and tulips rarely have a strong scent, but
Hyacinthus orientalis (common hyacinth), which develops
spires of waxlike, sweetly scented flowers during April and
May, is the perfect choice. The range of colors includes
white, yellow, pink, red, mauve, and blue. There are many
exciting combinations of plants with which they can be
used, including a medley of hyacinths, species tulips, and
yellow crocuses. In tubs and windowboxes, use pink
hyacinths, blue grape hyacinths, and yellow crocuses.

DELICIOUS DAPHNES

Daphnes are famed for their rich fragrance. Some start
flowering in late winter and continue into spring, while
others start in spring and continue into summer. Consider
the beautiful semievergreen or evergreen varieties *Daphne
blagayana*, *D. cneorum,* and *D. odora* 'Aureomarginata'.

SCENTED CHERRY TREES

Spring-flowering cherries are the epitome of spring, and
many have rich fragrances in addition to their flowers.
Prunus 'Amanogawa' (Lombard poplar cherry), a well-
known cherry with an upward stance, has slightly fragrant,
soft pink flowers during late April and into May, while *P. x
yedoensis* (Yoshino cherry) has nut-scented flowers from
March to April. Alternatively, *Prunus padus* 'Watereri' (bird
cherry), earlier known as *P. p.* 'Grandiflora', has drooping
tassels of almond-scented flowers during May.

A SPRING GARDEN

If your ambition is to plant a whole border or area of the
garden with plants specifically for spring, you might like
to try the garden design on the right.

Clematis montana *(mountain clematis), a vigorous deciduous climber, creates a wealth of sweetly scented, pure white flowers with a hint of vanilla in late spring.*

Hyacinthus orientalis *(common hyacinth) develops penetratingly sweet, upright spires of flowers in spring. There are many colors to choose from.*

Chamaecyparis lawsoniana *is a tall, dominant conifer, but there are a few slow-growing and miniature forms that are ideal for growing in tubs.*

Clematis armandii, *an evergreen climber, has saucer-shaped, pure white flowers in spring.*

Narcissus jonquilla *(wild jonquil) and* Muscari armeniacum *(grape hyacinth) create a scented color-contrast for spring.*

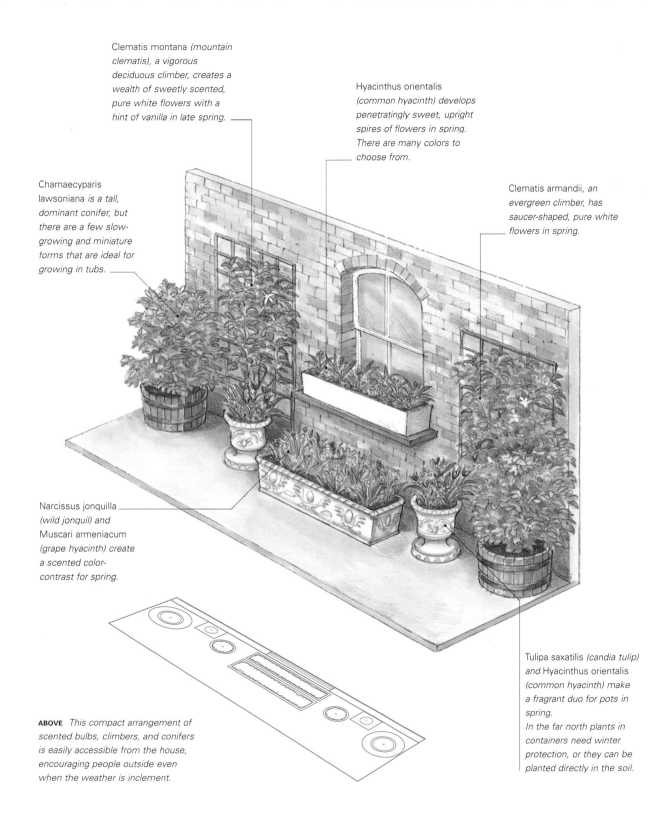

ABOVE *This compact arrangement of scented bulbs, climbers, and conifers is easily accessible from the house, encouraging people outside even when the weather is inclement.*

Tulipa saxatilis *(candia tulip) and* Hyacinthus orientalis *(common hyacinth) make a fragrant duo for pots in spring.*
In the far north plants in containers need winter protection, or they can be planted directly in the soil.

21

THE SCENTED SUMMER GARDEN

The warm, often balmy weather that floods summer creates a restful ambience. It also accentuates fragrances more than during cold weather. Some roses are richly scented, and several with unusual fragrances are described on pages 78–81. Many scented shrubs and trees (pages 82–91 and 100–105), as well as roses, are given a fresh dimension by planting them with companionable plants. Many of these arrangements are described here.

Opportunities abound during summer to plant scented shrubs and trees with companionable plants that either create additional fragrances or introduce further color. *Caryopteris* x *clandonensis*, a deciduous shrub with leaves that have a pungent aroma, develops bright blue flowers in late summer which can be contrasted against the variegated leaves of pampas grass. *Rhododendron luteum* has richly sweet, honey-scented flowers during May and June and is ideal for planting beside the lavender-blue-flowered *Primula vialii*. You might also consider planting the evergreen *Rosmarinus officinalis* alongside the deciduous shrub *Philadelphus coronarius* 'Aureus' to highlight the leaves and flowers of the former plant.

BELOW *Laburnum's common name is golden rain, which could hardly be more apt. Its flowers last until midsummer.*

SHRUBS AND TREES

To many gardeners, mock oranges are the epitome of early summer fragrance. Some, like *Philadelphus* 'Avalanche,' are ideal for small gardens, whereas others, like *P.* 'Beauclerk,' create more dominant features and would rather quickly outgrow a small site. Many of the taller-growing types are difficult to cohabit with other plants, but the smaller ones offer more opportunities.

Floriferous crab apples are popular deciduous trees that create a spectacle of color and scent in gardens. *Malus coronaria* 'Charlottae' is a magnificent, broad-headed tree that bears a profusion of violet-scented, semidouble, shell-pink flowers in large clusters at the end of May and into June. *M.* 'Profusion' has single, purple flowers that carry a light sweet fragrance, and are followed by small, oxblood-colored fruits.

LILIES

To many gardeners, fragrant lilies have near magical qualities, drenching borders in scent as well as revealing exquisitely shaped flowers. *Lilium candidum* (Madonna lily) has bell-shaped, pure white flowers during June and July that can be highlighted if it is grown against a background of purple-leaved shrubs such as *Cotinus coggygria* (smoke bush). Another effective combination is to plant it in front of several clumps of foxgloves, which have tall spires of thimblelike, purple-pink flowers. Blue delphiniums can also form an attractive background. Alternatively, for a simple yet impressive display, plant three or four lilies in a decorative pot for the patio.

A SUMMER GARDEN

If you would rather plant a whole border or area of the garden specifically with summer in mind, you might like to try the garden design on the right.

Jasminum x stephanense is a hybrid climber that grows well against a wall, producing clusters of fragrant pink flowers.

Rosa 'Madame Hardy', a Damask rose, creates a feast of lemon-scented, white flowers during midsummer. It is prickly, so take care.

Lonicera periclymenum (honeysuckle) is a superb climber with sweetly scented flowers during mid- and late summer.

Philadelphus 'Virginal' (mock orange) is a superb deciduous shrub with richly sweet white flowers during early and midsummer.

Buddleja fallowiana, a slightly tender deciduous shrub, creates a mass of sweetly scented flowers from midsummer to autumn.

Paeonia 'Sarah Bernhardt', a spectacular herbaceous perennial, has large, fragrant, double pink flowers in early and midsummer.

Lilium regale (regal or royal lily) produces spectacular white, sweetly scented, funnel-shaped flowers during midsummer.

Dianthus chinensis 'Frosted Mixed' is a border plant with an intensely sweet fragrance. It is ideal for the front of a border.

Romneya coulteri (tree poppy), a shrubby border plant, creates a mass of sweetly scented flowers from midsummer to autumn.

LEFT This massed border growing against a wall is packed with scented flowers and aromatic shrubs, which make an eye-catching display throughout much of the summer.

THE SCENTED AUTUMN GARDEN

Many plants continue their summer-flowering activities into the mists of autumn. They are ideal for bridging the massed and varied colors of summer and the eagerly anticipated brightness created by autumn-colored foliage. Many shrubs and climbers brighten autumn, while some bulbs also await the season of mellow fruitfulness to reveal their flowers. Bulbs usually flourish when planted around shrubs, where they gain protection from cold and blustery wind, as well as from frost.

Several fragrant shrubs that flower during mid- and late summer continue their display into autumn. *Buddleja davidii* (butterfly bush) produces long, tapering spires of lilac-purple flowers with a hint of honey and musk from July to October, while *Buddleja fallowiana* bears plumelike clusters of pale lavender-blue, sweetly scented flowers from July to September. Alternatively, *Ceanothus* 'Gloire de Versailles' produces spires of soft, powder-blue, sweetly scented flowers from June to October.

If you live in a coastal area, and salt-spray is a concern, *Elaeagnus* x *ebbingei*, an evergreen shrub with leathery leaves and sweetly scented, silvery flowers during October and November, is an excellent choice for autumn scent.

FLOWERING SHRUBS FOR AUTUMN COLOR

Several wall shrubs and climbers continue flowering into autumn. *Clematis flammula* (fragrant virgin's bower), a scrambling, deciduous climber, has white flowers that reveal a sweet and hawthornlike fragrance from August to October. *Clematis rehderiana*, a vigorous climber with bell-shaped, primrose-yellow flowers that reveal a light sweetness combined with a hint of cowslips, continues flowering from July to September.

If you love jasmine, *Jasminum officinale* (common white jasmine) is a lax and twining climber that has sweetly scented flowers from June to October. For the lover of honeysuckles, *Lonicera japonica* (Japanese honeysuckle) has sweet white to pale yellow flowers, with a hint of lemon, from June to October.

CORMS AND BULBS FOR AUTUMN

Several cormous plants create dainty, colorful, and fragrant displays in autumn. *Crocus sativus* (saffron crocus) has red-purple flowers with large red stigmas and a

ABOVE Lilium auratum *is an excellent choice of plant for sustaining a scented garden's* interest into autumn. Its pure white flowers drench the air in a richly sweet fragrance.

mosslike fragrance. *Cyclamen hederifolium* (earlier known as *C. neapolitanum*) develops faintly sweet flowers in a range of colors from white to pale pink and mauve, from August to November.

Lilies are often considered to be early to midsummer beauties, but many continue flowering into early autumn. Three of the best include *Lilium auratum* (golden-rayed lily), which produces strongly sweet, brilliant white flowers; *Lilium henryi*, a dominant plant with sweetly scented, pale apricot-yellow flowers with red spots; and *Lilium speciosum* (Japanese lily), which displays sweetly scented, white flowers. All three will flower from August through to September.

AN AUTUMN GARDEN

If you would like to plant a whole border or area of the garden with plants specifically with autumn in mind, you might like to try the garden design on the right.

Phlox paniculata *(summer or fall phlox) is a herbaceous perennial with a cluster of sweetly scented flowers from midsummer to early autumn.*

Clethra alnifolia *(sweet pepper bush) is a deciduous shrub with richly spicy flowers in late summer and early autumn.*

Elaeagnus x ebbingei, *an evergreen shrub with glossy, silver-gray leaves, bears silvery, creamy-white flowers in late autumn and into early winter.*

Cyclamen hederifolium *(still widely known as C. neapolitanum) creates a mass of fragrant flowers from late summer to early winter.*

Galtonia candicans *has lance-shaped gray-green leaves and produces bell-shaped white flowers in late summer and early autumn.*

Hosta plantaginea *(plantain lily) is a leafy border plant with tubular, highly fragrant white flowers during late summer and into early autumn.*

Cardiocrinum giganteum *(giant lily) creates a dramatic feature, with tall stems bearing cream or greenish-white flowers, mainly during mid- and late summer. The foliage remains attractive into early autumn.*

Monarda didyma *(bee balm), a herbaceous perennial, has green and hairy leaves that emit the redolence of bergamot, and bright scarlet flowers.*

LEFT *This oval bed has been planted so that its shrubs, bulbs, and perennials come into their own in the autumn, when other areas of the garden may be lacking color and interest.*

25

THE SCENTED WINTER GARDEN

*T*he cold and often dull months of winter need not be colorless or barren of attractive scents. Many scented shrubs and trees preempt spring with their rich and unusual fragrances, while from midwinter onward scented bulbs burst into color. These plants are best positioned near patios or firm-surfaced paths, from where their rich perfume can be readily appreciated. All winter-fragrant plants are a joy, and this can be enhanced further by combining plants in attractive groups.

Many of these winter-enriching shrubs and trees are described and illustrated on pages 82–91, and include *Chimonanthus* (wintersweet), *Hamamelis* (the witch hazels), mahonias, and several viburnums.

Underplant the spicily scented, December-to-February-flowering *Chimonanthus praecox* (wintersweet) with *Helleborus niger* (the Christmas rose). This evergreen border plant has saucer-shaped white flowers from December to March. For further color and scent add small clumps of *Galanthus nivalis* (the common snowdrop).

Alternatively, *Lonicera fragrantissima,* a honeysuckle that develops creamy-white, fragrant flowers from December to March, forms an appealing combination with the wintersweet and *Jasminum nudiflorum* (winter-flowering jasmine).

Consider also viburnums for your winter garden. These are superb shrubs and many enrich gardens with fragrance. *Viburnum farreri* has richly sweet, white flowers from November, followed by fruit.

Mahonias are ideal for planting in light shade under tall trees. *Mahonia japonica* has dark, glossy, leathery, spine-edged, and hollylike leaflets. The distinctively scented lemon-yellow flowers have the fragrance of lily-of-the-valley, and appear from January to March. They are borne in drooping clusters from the tips of the stems.

WINTER-FLOWERING BULBS

Some bulbs create their displays on the cusp of late winter and early spring. Many of these fragrant bulbs are described and illustrated on pages 70–73.

Crocus chrysanthus, a miniature bulb with rich golden-yellow, honey-scented flowers during late winter and into early spring, is ideal for naturalizing under white birches. For extra color, plant a range of varieties; they look superb when caught by the low rays of spring sunlight. The white bark adds extra sparkle to the scene.

Iris histrioides 'Major' bears rich royal-blue flowers with a delicate and sweet fragrance during January and February. It is ideal for planting in front of the *Jasminum nudiflorum* (winter-flowering jasmine), as well as with golden crocuses and white snowdrops. You could also consider *Iris reticulata,* which has violet-scented flowers during January and February, and is an ideal companion for *Galanthus nivalis,* which flowers in early winter.

A WINTER GARDEN

If your ambition is to plant a whole border or area of the garden with plants specifically for winter, you might like to try the garden design on the right.

BELOW *There is no reason for your garden to be bereft of scent during winter. The* strikingly scented mahonia family carry their scent from January through to March.

Viburnum farreri, *a deciduous shrub, reveals richly sweet flowers with a hint of heliotrope from early to late winter and sometimes into early spring.*

Mahonia japonica, *a spiny leaved evergreen shrub, bears clusters of flowers with the fragrance of lily-of-the-valley from mid-winter to early spring.*

Hamamelis japonica *(Japanese witch hazel), a spectacular deciduous shrub or small tree, bears spider-like, sweetly scented flowers from late winter to very early summer.*

Sarcococca humilis *(sweet box) is a small, tufted, clump-forming evergreen shrub with sweetly scented white flowers in late winter and into early spring.*

Daphne odora *'Aureomarginata' is an evergreen with mid-green leaves edged with cream. From midwinter to mid-spring it bears sweetly scented flowers.*

Galanthus nivalis *(common snowdrop) is a diminutive bulbous plant with nodding white flowers during midwinter and often into early spring.*

LEFT *Winter plantings can be surprisingly rich in scent and variety, as this corner bed reveals. They bring a touch of life to what may otherwise be a rather bare-looking scene. Plants described will bloom later in the north and earlier in the southern parts of their ranges.*

27

CREATING EVENING FRAGRANCE

Summer evenings have a magical quality, unsurpassed by any other time of day or year. There is a warm stillness that envelops a garden and strengthens the rich fragrances created by flowers and leaves. There are even some plants that are triggered into flower by the diminishing hours of daylight, while others, such as the four o'clock plant, start to reveal their scent during the retiring hours of an afternoon. Here is a range of plants that will bathe your garden in rich fragrance.

Many fragrant plants carry their scents into late evening, but there are a few that are especially famed for their evening and night scent. *Hesperis matronalis* (vesper flower or dame's violet), a short-lived perennial, has white, mauve, or purple flowers that during the day are practically scentless but in the evening give out a superb fragrance. *Matthiola bicornis* (night-scented stock) has purple-lilac flowers that reveal a heavy and sweet fragrance during evening and at night (*see page 62*). It has a sprawling and untidy nature, but this can be counteracted by sowing it in combination with the Virginian stock (*Malcolmia maritima*), another hardy annual. It has sweetly scented white flowers, borne amid gray-green leaves, and bears flowers four weeks after being sown, with flowering continuing for six to eight weeks. Other plants to consider are *Mirabilis jalapa* (four o'clock plant), *Nicotiana alata* (flowering tobacco plant), and *Oenothera biennis* (evening primrose), a biennial with primrose-yellow flowers that open during the evening and emit a sweet fragrance. As an added bonus, the seeds of this plant can be used to make evening primrose oil.

Several herbaceous perennials have a scent that is best appreciated after dusk. *Phlox maculata* (wild sweet William or meadow phlox) has tapering spires of intensely sweet purple flowers (*see page 68*) that are best appreciated in the evening, while *Saponaria officinalis* (common soapwort) has sweetly scented pink, red, or white flowers.

HONEYSUCKLE FOR EVENING FRAGRANCE
Honeysuckles are renowned for their sweetly fragrant flowers throughout the day and into evening; two choices described on page 77 are *Lonicera japonica* (Japanese honeysuckle) and *Lonicera periclymenum* 'Belgica', both with sweetly scented flowers.

ABOVE *Hidden among the erect stems of* Verbena bonariensis *are the delicately scented,* ghostly clusters of Nicotiana sylvestris, *which release their scent after dusk.*

SCENTED LILIES FOR POTS
Fragrant lilies in pots form exquisite features for patios and terraces and are easily accessible in the evening. Stem-rooting lilies for planting in pots include *Lilium auratum* (golden-rayed lily), which has brilliant white flowers with a sweet scent, and *Lilium speciosum* (Japanese lily), which bears white, bowl-shaped flowers that also carry a deliciously sweet scent.

AN EVENING GARDEN
If you would like to plant a whole border or area of the garden with evening-scented plants, you might like to try the garden design on the right.

Rosa 'Leverkusen', a climbing rose, develops lemon-yellow flowers with a distinctive lemon-like fragrance.

Daphne laureola (spurge laurel) is a bushy, evergreen shrub with intensely sweet, greenish-yellow flowers during late winter and into early spring.

Jasminum officinale has clusters of pure white, richly scented flowers from early summer to mid-autumn.

Hesperis matronalis (vesper flower), a short-lived perennial, has flowers with a strongly sweet and clove-scented fragrance, especially during the evening.

Osmanthus x burkwoodii, an evergreen shrub, creates a wealth of sweetly scented flowers during mid- and late spring.

Reseda odorata (mignonette) is a hardy annual with intensely sweet and musk-scented flowers.

Chamaecyparis pisifera 'Boulevard', a slow-growing conifer, has bright, blue-silver and green feathery foliage.

Oenothera biennis (evening primrose), a hardy biennial, has primrose-yellow flowers with a sweet fragrance in the evenings.

Choisya ternata (Mexican orange blossom) has leaves that emit the scent of orange when brushed.

LEFT Many flowers emit their fragrance most strongly during the evening. The scent from this terrace corner planted near the house will pervade the air.

CREATING YOUR GARDEN

2

Creating a scented garden is not difficult, and within this section we show just how easy it is. This covers choosing the type of plants required—from climbers for entrances and trellises to those that create color and fragrance in containers on patios—to buying, propagating, and looking after scented plants. There is also information on creating specific features, from fragrant water gardens to scented bowers.

LEFT *Not all water lilies (Nymphaea spp.) are fragrant, but those that are have a rich perfume. The tall, umbrella-like heads of the flowering rush (Butomus umbellatus) can be seen at the front of the pond.*

SCENTED CLIMBERS • CHOICES

❶ ENTRANCES

Doorways surrounded by fragrant climbers produce a restful and friendly approach to homes. Many of the less vigorous scented roses on pages 80–81 can be used to enhance entrances, while the large-flowered types have the appropriate vigor to cover a wall on one side of a door without eventually producing a jungle of stems and leaves.

Rustic entrances need the informality provided by the lax and floriferous honeysuckles. Either the early Dutch honeysuckle (*Lonicera periclymenum* 'Belgica') or Japanese honeysuckle (*L. japonica* 'Halliana') is superb.

CHOICE CHECKLIST

∾ Prune *L. periclymenum* back to strong young growth soon after bloom each year.
∾ Shrubs trained against a wall are easier to constrain than rapid-growing climbers.

∾ If possible, climbers should slightly intrude over the outer edge of a door frame, to integrate the climber with the entrance.

Pathfinder *see pages 76–77, 80–81* →

❷ ARCHES, ARBORS, AND PERGOLAS

Formal arches and pergolas have a regular nature that suits many modern gardens, where straight borders and paths are dominant. Formal pergolas are ideal for supporting wisterias, climbers like *Akebia quinata* and *Clematis montana*, although unless large these supports can become encapsulated with foliage and flowers.

Rustic variations have a soft and informal nature perfect for older gardens. They are superb when clothed with scented climbers such as *Clematis flammula*, *C. rehderiana*, *Jasminum officinale*, and floriferous honeysuckles which have a wonderful informal nature.

CHOICE CHECKLIST

∾ As well as growing sprawling climbers over arches, consider training a flowering tree over an arch.
∾ If someone in the family has impaired vision, do not

plant thorned climbers over arches straddling a path.
∾ Bear in mind that several scented clematis develop attractive seedheads which last well into winter.

Pathfinder *see pages 76–77, 80–81* →

❸

TRELLIS SCREENS

Trellises are usually attached to walls (as above); an alternative is to create a free-standing screen formed of trellis panels secured to strong posts. They are ideal for creating privacy as well as separating one part of a garden from another. In areas where winter wind is strong and blustery, use deciduous climbers that do not produce a strong barrier. *Clematis montana* and large-flowered clematis have a semiformal nature ideal for town gardens, while *C. flammula* and *C. rehderiana* reveal an informal nature and are really better suited to a relaxed country-garden setting.

The popular annual sweet pea (*Lathyrus odoratus*) is ideal for informal screens, and varieties and colors can be changed from one season to another.

CHOICE CHECKLIST	
❧ A freestanding trellis should have a space of 15–18in (38–45cm) between itself and any boundary fence to prevent intrusion into next-door's plot.	❧ In exposed areas, make the trellis more stable by erecting a 2–2½ft (60–75cm) long piece of trellis at a right angle to its end.

Pathfinder *see pages 76–77* →

❹

WALLS

Most houses offer space for climbers and shrubs trained against a wall. Scented climbers growing against a wall usually need support from a trellis or wires attached to the brickwork. Ensure the wall is sound and that the trellis is well secured. For a large wall, wisterias have few rivals and create a wealth of vanilla-scented flowers during late spring. The deciduous shrub *Abeliophyllum distichum* is better suited to small walls, as is the evergreen *Azara microphylla*. *Cytisus battandieri* is also suited to walls, especially old types and those with a relaxed and informal nature. For winter color plant *Viburnum farreri*, which has clusters of white flowers that are tinged pink when in bud.

CHOICE CHECKLIST	
❧ For red brick walls, select mainly white, blue, silver, or soft yellow flowers. ❧ For white walls, select mainly climbers with yellow, gold, or scarlet flowers.	Blue and mauve flowers also look good. ❧ For gray stone walls select plants with deep purple, deep blue, pink, or red flowers.

Pathfinder *see pages 48–49, 76–77, 82* →

SCENTED PATIOS AND TERRACES • CHOICES

❶

HANGING BASKETS AND WALL BASKETS

Hanging baskets create focal points at eye-level. They are ideal for small garden areas, because they make use of "dead" space, and help to bring a three-dimensional aspect to the patio garden. Solid-sided baskets (which are really suspended pots) have become popular because they dry out less quickly than wire-framed baskets, but they cannot be planted to give the same "all-around" effect as a traditional basket. Brackets can be mounted on walls, pillars, and posts; they can also be suspended from the overhead beams of pergolas. Even at a low level, baskets can make an attractive feature. Wall baskets are ideal for securing to walls and are especially suitable for positions where a patio or other paved surface abuts a wall.

CHOICE CHECKLIST

❧ Use hanging baskets to bring color to bland walls, alone or in combination with wall baskets.

❧ Position on either side of a window, securing them so the foliage slightly interrupts the window's vertical edges.
❧ Use either side of a wall basket or a trough.

Pathfinder *see pages 38–39, 42–43* ➜

❷

SCENTED WINDOWBOXES

Throughout the year, delicious fragrances can be created in windowboxes.

The best way to create such displays is by having an ornate outer windowbox, into which three successive plastic troughs can be put and removed throughout the year. In autumn, remove the summer display and replace it with a winter display, formed of miniature conifers and small bulbs. In late winter, remove the winter display and put in its place a spring display, planted up in autumn and formed of biennials and spring-flowering bulbs. In early summer, remove this and replace with a display formed of scented annuals and perennials.

CHOICE CHECKLIST

❧ Windowboxes used to brighten sash-windows can be placed directly on the sill.
❧ Windowboxes used with windows that open outward must be secured to the wall

below the level of the window's sill. This also applies to many modern double-glazed windows.

Pathfinder *see pages 38–39, 42–43* ➜

❸

OLD WHEELBARROWS AND TROUGHS

Old wheelbarrows, whether constructed of wood or metal, can be made secure and planted with summer-flowering scented plants. In spring, clean up and paint the wheelbarrow, check that drainage holes in its base are open, fill with soil, and plant with scented plants.

Troughs are an ideal way to bring color to the tops of walls. If two brackets are fixed to the sides of a wall, a trough can be positioned on them. Troughs and other containers on patios, as well as on balconies, can be packed with scented plants to create both spring and summer displays. Bulbs are ideal for spring displays.

CHOICE CHECKLIST	
❧ Wheelbarrows are best reserved for large colorful summer-flowering plants. ❧ Plant the wheelbarrow where it is to remain throughout summer.	❧ Troughs can be positioned along the edge of flat roofs, where they will soften harsh edges, but be sure to avoid blocking gutters.

Pathfinder *see pages 38–39* ➜

❹

WOODEN CASKS AND OTHER CONTAINERS

A wooden wine cask is easily turned into a plant container by cutting out a window on one side and mounting it on legs or bricks. Drill holes in its base, add drainage material and then fill with soil. This sort of container is ideal for growing a range of summer-flowering plants.

If you don't have a wine cask, tubs, pots, urns, and even car tires provide homes for many types of plants, from shrubs to annuals, during summer. Good drainage and clean soil are essential. Alternatively, the versatile growing-bag is an inexpensive yet attractively rustic way of displaying spring-flowering bulbs. Plant them in autumn and place in their flowering positions.

CHOICE CHECKLIST	
❧ Be thrifty and reuse growing-bags used during the previous year in a greenhouse. Liven up the soil with a sprinkling of fresh fertilizer.	❧ Stand wooden tubs on three bricks to raise them off the ground; this ensures adequate drainage. Allowing plants to stand in water can cause considerable damage.

Pathfinder *see pages 38–39, 70–73* ➜

TYPES OF SCENTED GARDENS • CHOICES

❶

COUNTRY GARDENS

Country gardens have a relaxed, soft, and informal nature. This style does not suit all houses, but even where a house is modern a small area can often be set aside for a country-garden feature. If the area is backed by fragrant, informal climbers, such as honeysuckle and jasmine, this helps to foster an even more relaxed ambience.

The range of scented country-garden plants for summer color is wide and includes hardy annuals such as *Scabiosa atropurpurea* (sweet scabious) and *Centaurea moschata* (sweet sultan). The short-lived perennial *Hesperis matronalis* (vesper flower) is superb, as well as the longer-lived *Dictamnus albus* (burning bush). Many scented lilies have a relaxed nature and these are featured on pages 72–73.

CHOICE CHECKLIST

∾ Grow herbs among herbaceous perennials, annuals, and shrubs.
∾ Plant an apple tree in a flower border to create height and extra interest.

∾ Gooseberries and currants are superb country-garden fruits that can be grown as cordons as well as bushes.

Pathfinder *see pages 48–49, 60–63* ➜

❷

WILD GARDENS

Wild gardens are not unkempt and neglected features, but areas of organized informality, usually in the light shade created by a canopy of deciduous trees, such as birches. The dappled light in spring produces ideal conditions for early-flowering bulbs, while later in the year, when the sunlight is stronger, the leafy branches ensure indirect light for a wide range of plants that prefer partial shade.

Several scented bulbous plants produce spectacular displays, including *Lilium hansonii*, polyanthus and primroses, deciduous azaleas, cormous plants such as *Cyclamen repandum* (mainly spring flowering) and *Convallaria majalis* (lily-of-the-valley). These plants, which saturate the air with scent, are ideal for spring displays.

CHOICE CHECKLIST

∾ Log steps are ideal features for sloping paths in a wild garden.
∾ Protect newly planted bulbs from mice by covering with pieces of wire-netting.

∾ Logs used to form edges to beds help to prevent soil and mulching materials being scattered by rains.

Pathfinder *see pages 70–73* ➜

❸

TOWN GARDENS

These gardens usually need resilient plants, able to withstand buffeting from wind whipping around a corner or channeled between buildings. The warmth of summer is often intensified by buildings and soil close to them quickly becomes dry. Many shrubs and trees tolerate these conditions, while a medley of herbaceous perennials, bulbs, biennials, and annuals create color from spring to autumn. In small gardens, scented plants in containers are invaluable. Windowboxes provide homes for plants throughout the year. Do not use hanging baskets in gardens tormented by strong summer winds, as plants soon become damaged, the soil dries rapidly, and supporting chains and brackets are weakened.

CHOICE CHECKLIST

❧ Ferns are welcome additions, especially where the soil is moist and shaded.
❧ Use small, nonrampant climbers and narrow upright trees in small gardens.

❧ Low, hummock-forming grasses are ideal for low-maintenance gardens.

Pathfinder *see pages 34–35, 42–43* ➜

❹

FORMAL GARDENS

Formal gardens have a regimented and clinical nature that appeals to many gardeners. Bulbs and biennials are used to create spring displays, while annuals are ideal for summer. Exotic-looking tender perennial plants can be interspersed among the lower-growing, carpet-forming plants.

Beds alongside paths and lawns can be brightened by mixing many color-contrasting plants. A less regimented scented display can be achieved by planting the scented *Heliotropium arborescens* with the silver-leaved *Senecio cineraria*. Spring-flowering displays using tulips planted amid a sea of *Erysimum* x *allionii* (earlier and still better known as *Cheiranthus* x *allionii*, and popularly as wall-flowers) create memorable features.

CHOICE CHECKLIST

❧ Use urns on pedestals to create height and drama.
❧ Regularly shaped, round containers suit formal plants with a symmetrical outline.

❧ Square, wooden, Versailles-type containers are ideal for plants with regular outlines.
❧ Consider using box or yew to create striking topiary features for a patio garden.

Pathfinder *see pages 60–63, 70–73* ➜

BUYING SCENTED PLANTS

*T*he range of fragrant plants is wide and includes shrubs, trees, conifers, bulbs, herbaceous
perennials, annuals, and half-hardy annuals. Most are widely available from garden
centers and nurseries, but some plants, especially bulbs, are also bought through specialty
catalogs in autumn. Buying by mail order will give you a much wider range of available
plants, and if you buy in quantity you can share with a friend.

Shrubs, and especially trees, form the main framework of
a scented garden, and therefore they must be thoroughly
checked to ensure that they are healthy and able to create
a long-term display. Herbaceous perennials are less long-
lived and usually need to be lifted and divided every three
or four years. Plants such as half-hardy annuals, which are
bought in spring, can become expensive, especially when
several boxes of them are needed. It is possible to sow them
yourself in early spring, in gentle warmth in a greenhouse
or conservatory.

There are several sources of scented plants, including
garden centers, local nurseries, specialty nurseries, florists,
and through mail-order catalogs.

GARDEN CENTERS AND NURSERIES

Garden centers are popular because plants can be seen
before they are bought, but the range may be limited. Since
their inception in the 1960s, garden centers have grown
and sold shrubs, trees, climbers, and many other plants in
containers. These can be planted whenever the soil and
weather allow. Before the 1960s, deciduous trees, shrubs,
and hedging plants were sold as bare-rooted plants during
their dormant period, while evergreens had their roots
wrapped in burlap and were sold mainly in late spring.

General and specialist nurseries offer a wide range of
plants and often issue catalogs. Like garden centers, they
offer plants for sale in containers, but unlike most garden
centers they usually raise their own plants instead of
buying them in for resale. Some nurseries are not always
open to the general public, so before making a visit tele-
phone to find out their openhours. Many nurseries provide

HINTS AND TIPS

🌿 Check that bulbs are firm and heavy for their size. Bulbs
that are large and heavy are likely to flower well.

🌿 Check that bulbs have their tunic (a thin papery layer)
intact, although some splitting is normal. Therefore, in
practical terms avoid those where most of the papery
covering is missing.

🌿 Check that the bulbs are free from molds and insects. If
present, these usually congregate around the neck or base.
Similarly, check that they are not infected with diseases.

🌿 Avoid very large tubers, as they may not be as good as
small ones; large and old tubers are sometimes reluctant to
develop shoots.

LEFT *Garden centers and
nurseries carry a range of
plants, but more unusual
types may not be available.
Ensure plants are properly
labeled before purchasing.*

TECHNIQUE **SELECTING PLANTS IN CONTAINERS**

1 The soil in the container must be moist but not waterlogged. If excessively wet, the roots may have started to rot; if too dry, they will also have suffered.

2 If moss is present on the surface of the soil, this is a warning that the plant has been neglected and has been kept in the container for too long.

3 Check that masses of roots are not protruding out of the container's drainage holes. This indicates that the plant is pot bound. Plants seldom fully recover if the roots are excessively matted.

4 Check that the plant has not been recently potted up for a quick sale. Unfortunately, this state often cannot be detected until the planting. Make sure too that the plant is clearly labeled.

POINTS TO CONSIDER

- Bulbs (including corms and tubers) are available from garden centers as well as through mail-order catalogs, which are usually sent out during late summer. Some catalogs arrive unsolicited through the mail, while specialty bulb companies have to be contacted for unusual bulbs, corms, and tubers.
- Toward the end of the bulb-planting season (mainly from late summer to early autumn), bulbs are often offered at reduced prices. These can be good buys if you do not mind taking a bit of a gamble, but check the bulbs carefully before buying them. Do not worry too much if they have started to sprout, but avoid any that appear to be soft or showing signs of disease.
- Do not throw away hyacinth bulbs that have been grown indoors for flowering at Christmas or in late winter. After the flowers fade, gradually reduce the amount of water that they are given and place in a cool, frostproof, well-lit location. When all the foliage has died down—and after all risk of frost has passed—plant them outdoors in a shrub or flower border.

a mail-order service; sometimes there is a minimum charge to cover packaging and shipping (this will be indicated in the catalog).

PLANT SHOPS

Many shops, from florists to greengrocers, now sell plants. Even some of the larger supermarkets have started stocking a limited range of species. In spring these are mainly half-hardy bedding plants. Do not plant them out until all risk of frost has passed. Before planting them, stand the containers on a well-drained surface and water the soil thoroughly.

MARKET PLACES AND LOCAL PLANT SALES

These offer plants mainly in spring and early summer and, while bargains can often be had, always check that the plants are healthy and have a well-established root-system. Also check that pests and diseases are not present; the plants are more likely to be infected than those bought from professional outlets such as garden centers and nurseries. If you suspect that pests are present, spray the plant when you get it home and isolate it until you are quite certain that it is healthy. This especially applies to greenhouse and conservatory plants, where pests such as whitefly and red spider mites can spread rapidly.

PROPAGATING SCENTED PLANTS

The range of scented plants that can easily be propagated is wide and encompasses popular plants such as hardy and half-hardy annuals, shrubs, and herbaceous perennials. Apart from saving you money, there is a wealth of satisfaction in successfully raising your own plants. Growing from seed also means that you can grow the precise varieties you desire and not have to rely on the frequently limited range available at garden centers. Coordinate with friends so that you can exchange trays of different seedlings.

Hardy annuals can be sown outdoors in the positions where the plants will grow and flower, without having to be germinated first in a greenhouse. In one season they germinate from seeds and produce flowers before dying with the onset of cold weather in autumn.

Scented hardy annuals include *Iberis amara* (candytuft), *Limnanthes douglasii* (poached egg plant), *Malcolmia maritima* (Virginian stock), *Matthiola bicornis* (night-scented stock), *Reseda odorata* (mignonette), *Scabiosa atropurpurea* (sweet scabious), and *Centaurea moschata* (sweet sultan). These

TECHNIQUE   **SOWING HARDY ANNUALS**

1 Dig the soil in winter and remove perennial weeds. Leave the surface rough but level, so by spring, frost, snow, and rain will have created a fine tilth. In spring, rake the surface.

2 Prepare for seed sowing by systematically shuffling sideways over the soil's surface. Do not use a roller, as invariably it is too heavy and can leave you with uneven surfaces.

WATCHPOINTS

❧ Never take cuttings from plants that are wilting. If the mother plant is in a pot, first water the soil.
❧ When transplanting biennials to a nursery bed or their flowering positions, water them during the previous day. Also water the planting area.
❧ Never take cuttings from pest- or disease-infected plants.
❧ When sowing seeds in the garden, sow them thinly and evenly. Congested seedlings are prone to diseases. Additionally, they will have to compete unnecessarily for light, air, and food.
❧ When dividing herbaceous perennials, do not split them into exceptionally small pieces, as the plants then take several seasons to create a good display.

3 Sketch the shape of the proposed bed on paper to indicate the sowing areas. Transfer the plan to the border, using either a pointed stick or a narrow line of sharp sand.

4 Form shallow furrows, about ¼ in (6mm) deep and 6–8in (15– 20cm) apart, using a pointed stick guided by a straight-edge board, garden line, or the back of a metal rake.

5 Sow seeds evenly and thinly. Sowing thickly encourages disease and is a waste of money. Do not sow during blustery spells, or if the soil is very wet or dry.

6 When sowing is complete, use the back of a metal rake to push friable soil over the seeds. Use the head of the rake when the handle is vertical to firm the soil.

1 Fill a clean seed-tray with seed starter soil and firm with your fingers, especially around the edges. This area becomes dry first if the soil is not sufficiently compacted and watering is subsequently neglected. Use a "firmer"—a piece of flat wood with a handle—to firm the surface.

2 Tip the seeds into a piece of paper that has been folded to form a V-shape and sprinkle thinly and evenly over the surface by tapping the paper. Do not sow within ½in (12mm) of the container's sides. Most seeds germinate in darkness, so cover them lightly with fine soil using a sieve.

3 Water the soil by placing the seed-tray in a large bowl shallowly filled with water, and then place a transparent lid over the seed-tray to help conserve moisture in the soil and to create a uniform temperature. Also, cover with a sheet of newspaper until the seeds germinate.

annuals look attractive sown in small groups in beds under windows or, alternatively, in large borders where they create a more dramatic display.

SOWING HALF-HARDY ANNUALS

Half-hardy annuals should be sown in gentle warmth (61–70°F/16–21°C) in greenhouses and conservatories in late winter or early spring. Once the seeds germinate and the seedlings are growing strongly, transfer them to wider and uniform spacings in a seed-tray, where they will develop into healthy plants. They need to acclimatize slowly to outdoor conditions, and when all risk of frost has passed they can be planted into borders or containers.

Scented half-hardy annuals include *Brachyscome iberidifolia* (Swan River daisy), *Heliotropium arborescens* (heliotrope), *Matthiola incana* (stock), *Mirabilis jalapa* (four o'clock plant), *Nemesia caerulea*, *Nicotiana alata* (flowering tobacco plant), and *Verbena* x *hybrida* (verbena).

DIVIDING HERBACEOUS PERENNIALS

The division of congested clumps of herbaceous perennials is a quick and easy way to propagate them. This usually needs to be done every three or four years and is a task best tackled in the dormant period of early spring, although in mild areas autumn is also suitable.

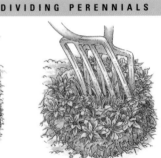

1 Carefully dig up a congested clump, and place it gently on the border soil.

2 To divide the clump, insert two garden forks, back to back, in the clump's center.

3 Move the handles of the forks together to separate the entangled roots. When these are loose, pull the forks apart.

4 Use your hands to pull plants apart, keeping only young pieces from the edges. These can be planted into a border.

CARE AND MAINTENANCE

Scented plants need the same dedicated care and attention as other plants, whether in borders, flower beds, or containers on patios and terraces. Neglected plants, whether shrubs, roses, herbaceous perennials, or annuals, create dismal displays. Incidentally, summer-flowering bedding plants in containers such as hanging baskets, windowboxes, troughs, and tubs need more attention than shrubs in borders. Climbers also need attention, especially when young and before they are growing strongly.

Regular inspection of plants in containers is essential if you are to get the best from them. During summer, plants need to be watered about twice a day. Adding moisture-retentive materials to the soil in hanging baskets, as well as using moisture-retentive liners, also helps. Regularly feeding and spraying plants helps them to create an attractive display throughout summer. Finally, frequently check both flowering plants and those grown for their attractive leaves for dead flowers and damaged leaves.

CHANGING PLANTS

Sometimes plants are put directly into soil in a windowbox. This may mean changing plants, which can often be a trying experience. If, however, you leave plants in their pots and just stand them in a windowbox, new plants can easily be exchanged for those that are past their best.

1 Feed plants in containers regularly throughout the summer, using a fertilizer dissolved in water. Apply this every ten to fourteen days. Never apply fertilizer to dry soil, as it will damage the roots of plants.

2 Because plants are packed together in containers, they provide convenient meals for pests. Inspect plants regularly and use an environmentally friendly spray that will not harm the earth. But first, pick off any dead flowers.

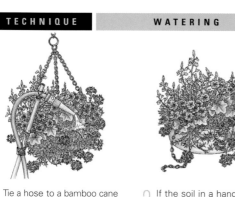 

1 Tie a hose to a bamboo cane to trickle water into a hanging basket. Commercial attachments are available to enable you to water windowboxes and hanging baskets more easily.

2 If the soil in a hanging basket becomes very dry, take down the basket and stand it in a large bowl of water. Leave it immersed until bubbles cease to rise from the soil.

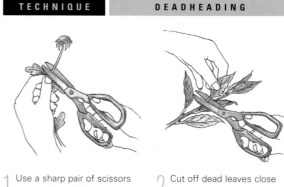

1 Use a sharp pair of scissors to cut off dead flowers, complete with the stem. Cut the stem just above a leaf joint. Remove the flowers and place them on a compost heap.

2 Cut off dead leaves close to their base. Check regularly that the soil is moist. Both leaves and flowers suffer if the soil is allowed to become dry.

HINTS AND TIPS

HINTS AND TIPS

🌿 In early spring, refirm soil around herbaceous perennials planted during the previous autumn. The soil may have been loosened by frost.

🌿 In spring, shallowly fork between plants to break up a crusty surface; this will enable air and water to enter the soil.

🌿 In late spring or early summer, dust the surface with a general fertilizer. Shallowly hoe this into the surface soil, then thoroughly water the entire area.

🌿 After feeding and watering plants, form a 2–3in (5–7.5cm) thick mulch of compost between the plants, ensuring first that the soil is moist and free of any weeds..

🌿 In autumn, cut down herbaceous perennials to ground level and rake debris from the surface. Cutting down the plants can be delayed until late winter.

TECHNIQUE   **WEEDING**

1 It is safer to weed by hand, but this is often impractical for large beds and borders. Hoes can be used but may accidentally damage plants. Remember to remove the roots of perennial weeds as well as the visible part.

2 Once a bed has been weeded, cover with a mulch. Well-rotted organic material such as manure or garden compost is ideal, and composted bark chippings are also excellent. Apply a layer 2–3in (5–7.5cm) deep.

WEEDING THE SCENTED GARDEN

The regular removal of weeds is essential. If perennial weeds are removed when the soil is prepared, you stand a much better chance of keeping the soil free from unwanted plants. The second point to remember is to weed during winter if at all possible. Warm weather is a time of rapid growth for weeds as well as other plants!

PESTS AND DISEASES

Wherever plants grow in the garden, there will always be pests and diseases waiting to attack them. Sometimes the effects of these are very minor; at other times they can just be devastating.

Infestations of aphids can sometimes be washed off with a strong jet of water. There are many chemicals available which are specific to aphids.

Irregular holes chewed in leaves are often a sign of caterpillars. If you have the patience, large caterpillars can be picked off by hand and destroyed.

Scale insects are sap-sucking pests that look like small limpets attached to stems and the undersides of leaves; they exude a sticky honeydew on which sooty mold may grow. They can be scraped off by hand if you have the patience. Scale insects are difficult to control with chemicals.

Slugs and snails can be a serious nuisance. Hand picking with a flashlight after dark can be productive but unpleasant, or organic controls such as traps filled with beer may help.

Vine weevils are an increasingly common problem with container-grown plants. The adult weevils eat notches out of foliage, but it is the larvae, however, that cause the most problems. They live in the soil and eat plant roots, often escaping detection until the plant collapses and dies. A biological control is available, and soil insecticides can be applied to the soil.

Powdery mildew is common on plants such as Michaelmas daisies, particularly if they are overcrowded. Spray affected plants with a general fungicide. Clear up and destroy all affected growth at the end of the season to prevent spores overwintering.

Pale spots on the upper surface of leaves and concentric brown rings on the undersides indicate rust. Remove and destroy affected leaves as soon as you notice them and spray with a suitable fungicide.

Viruses cause a wide range of symptoms, from yellow mottling to crinkled leaf edges. Viruses are impossible to treat, and badly affected plants must be removed and destroyed. Many viruses are spread by aphids, so keeping these pests under control is the simplest and most effective way to prevent infection of plants.

SUPPORTING AND PRUNING PLANTS

Caring for scented plants often involves supporting and pruning. If you have the room to grow a tree it may require some form of support in its early years. Not all herbaceous perennials need staking; some are self-supporting and are ideal for planting in an "island" bed. Another technique you will need to have in your repertoire is pruning, a simple and logical process that will bring many benefits to your garden.

Herbaceous perennials are plants that each year develop fresh shoots in spring and produce flowers during summer. In autumn, many plants die down to soil level. Some herbaceous plants are self-supporting. Those that do need help can be supported in three different ways (*see below right*). Insert supports while plants are still small, so that stems and leaves grow up and through them.

Trees may be staked at the same time as they are planted (doing it later can damage the roots). Strong winter winds can loosen their roots in the soil and prevent rapid establishment. Three methods of giving support are shown on the opposite page.

PRUNING DECIDUOUS SHRUBS

Deciduous shrubs shed their leaves in autumn and develop fresh ones in spring. Some of these shrubs need regular pruning in order to encourage the yearly development of flowers. Shrubs that are grown in temperate climates can be divided up into three main flowering periods: winter-flowering, spring- and early summer-flowering, and late summer-flowering.

Winter-flowering shrubs are the easiest to prune: simply cut out damaged, crossing, or diseased shoots in spring. Spring- and early summer-flowering shrubs are pruned immediately after their flowers fade. Cut out the shoots that produced flowers, as well as thin, spindly, and diseased shoots; also thin out the shoots to encourage light and air to circulate. Late summer-flowering shrubs are pruned in spring, rather than immediately after their flowers fade.

PRUNING EVERGREEN SHRUBS

Established evergreen shrubs need little pruning other than cutting out weak and diseased shoots in spring. Frost-damaged shoots and leaves may also need to be removed. In very cold areas, wait until early summer. If a shrub flowers in spring, delay pruning until the flowers have faded.

WATCHPOINTS

ﾟ Cold winter and spring winds damage young trees and shrubs. Form a temporary burlap screen on the windward side, but do not completely enclose a plant.
ﾟ Vertical stakes should not be inserted into the root ball, or the roots may be damaged.
ﾟ During the first few months, check the tree regularly to ensure that the trunk is not being restricted by tight tree ties or tying materials.

TECHNIQUE   SUPPORTING HERBACEOUS PERENNIALS

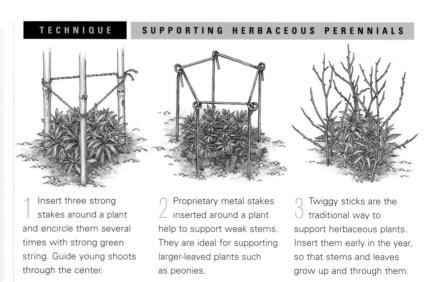

1 Insert three strong stakes around a plant and encircle them several times with strong green string. Guide young shoots through the center.

2 Proprietary metal stakes inserted around a plant help to support weak stems. They are ideal for supporting larger-leaved plants such as peonies.

3 Twiggy sticks are the traditional way to support herbaceous plants. Insert them early in the year, so that stems and leaves grow up and through them.

TECHNIQUE   **VERTICAL STAKE**

1 Dig out the planting hole and then pound in the stake. Position the stake on the wind-ward side of the tree, with the top just below the lowest branch. Spread out the tree's roots, cover with soil, and firm it.

2 Then, secure the trunk to the stake in at least two places. About six months later, recheck the "ties" to ensure that they are secure but not strangling the trunk. Repeat this every year.

TECHNIQUE   **OBLIQUE AND H-STAKE**

1 Using this method, the stake is inserted after the tree has been planted. It is an ideal staking method if a tree has to be restaked after the original one breaks. The stake's top must face the prevailing wind.

1 This type of stake is inserted after a tree has been planted and often as a remedial method if a tree's first stake should fail. Check regularly that the trunk is not constricted and that the stakes are secure.

TECHNIQUE   **BASIC PRUNING**

1 Thin shoots should be cut with sharp pruning shears. Prune with a cut that starts just above a bud and slopes back at a slight angle.

2 Do not cut too close to or too far away from a bud. In the latter case, the long piece of stem above the bud forms a "snag", which dies back and can kill the main stem.

3 Use a saw for larger branches, first cutting a quarter of the way through from the underside of the branch, 6–9in (15–23cm) from the trunk.

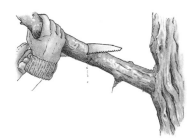

4 Make another cut about 1in (2.5cm) further out along the branch, this time cutting right through. These first two cuts are to remove the weight of the branch.

5 Move to your final position and cut straight through the branch. This final cut removes the rest of the branch without the problem of the weight pulling down.

6 Pare away rough edges around the cut. It is not essential to coat the cut's surface with a fungicidal paint, but it makes it look more attractive.

CREATING A SCENTED SHRUB BORDER

Shrubs and trees form a permanent framework in gardens around which other plants can be positioned. Additionally, trees such as **Prunus padus** *'Waterei', which has almond-scented flowers, are ideal as a focal point in a large lawn. If you only have space in your garden for a few scented shrubs, position them alongside paths or at the edges of a patio, where their fragrances are quickly and easily appreciated. It will then be possible to gently rub their leaves as you pass to reveal their scent.*

Many shrubs have leaves that have unusual fragrances. Plants native to warm countries are especially rich in scents, and these range from *Choisya ternata* (Mexican orange blossom) to *Cistus ladanifer* (gum cistus) from Mediterranean regions, which has dull green, leathery leaves that exude a richly sweet gum. Laudanum, a heavily fragrant oil used in the preparation of some perfumes, is distilled from this gum. Many other cistus shrubs have aromatic leaves, and they all produced beautiful flowers during the summer months.

The wide range of fragrances produced by shrubs that have aromatic leaves is most noticeable during warm, sunny periods, when the heat of the sun readily vaporizes their oils to reveal their scent. Conversely, the majority of

---

PROJECT | **A SCENTED SHRUB BORDER**

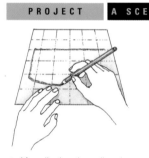

1 After digging the soil and removing perennial weeds, it is essential to plan the positions of the shrubs. Measure and carefully draw to scale on paper.

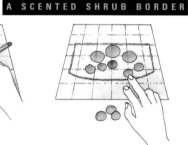

2 Use colored pieces of paper cut to the same scale as the border, to represent the size of each shrub when it is grown. Also indicate heights.

STAR PLANTS

The following plants are suitable for a scented hedge.

- Tall hedges—over 6ft (1.8m) high
  Chamaecyparis lawsoniana
  Thuja plicata
- Medium hedges—2–6ft (60cm–1.8m) high
  Elaeagnus x ebbingei
  Rosa 'Buff Beauty'
  Rosmarinus officinalis
- Low hedges—8–15in (20–45cm) high
  Hyssopus officinalis
  Santolina chamaecyparissus

3 Mark positions on the soil, using dry sand. Place the shrubs in position and inspect from several angles.

4 The day before planting, water the shrubs and check that the soil in the border is moist; water, if necessary.

5 Dig out a hole 12in (30cm) wider than the container's width, and slightly deeper. Firm a mound of soil in the base.

6 Insert the soil-ball, then use a trowel to draw friable soil around it. Firm in layers, mulch, then water thoroughly.

PROJECT   PLANTING A SCENTED HEDGE

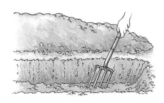

1 Dig a trench about 12in (30cm) deep and 12–18in (30–45cm) wide where the hedge is to be sited. Fork over the base to ensure that it is not compacted, and check that all perennial weeds have been removed.

2 The day before planting the hedge, water the plants. Place them, still in their containers, on a well-drained surface, and thoroughly moisten the soil. Allow excess water to drain away.

3 Stand the plants, still in their pots, in the trench, and use a straight-edged piece of wood to check that the surface of the soil-ball is slightly below the surrounding soil. This allows for later soil settlement.

4 Remove the containers and space the plants 18–24in (45–60cm) apart. Draw soil around the soil-balls and firm it in layers. Then, gently use the heel of your shoe to firm the soil level with the surrounding ground.

5 Insert a strong bamboo cane on the windward side of each stem. Tie the stem to the cane, but ensure that it is not constricted. Regularly check the stem, because soil settlement during the following weeks may cause strangulation.

6 Thoroughly water the area to ensure that soil particles are in close contact with the roots. Repeated watering will be necessary until the plants start to grow, especially if the weather is dry. Also, add a mulch over the soil.

coniferous shrubs are native to cool regions, and those with aromatic foliage need gentle rubbing to encourage them to release their scent.

Some of the most popular garden shrubs with aromatic leaves include *Caryopteris* x *clandonensis*, *Choisya ternata*, *Cistus ladanifer*, *Gaultheria procumbens*, lavender, *Ruta graveolens*, rosemary, and thymes. Details of these can be found in the plant directory (*see pages 100–103*).

PLANTING A SCENTED HEDGE

A scented lavender hedge, or one formed of fragrant roses (*see pages 78–79* for suitable varieties), creates a superb feature. These plants are ideal as small, perhaps internal hedges, whereas one formed of conifers creates a bolder barrier against wind. Several of the conifers described on pages 104–105 are suitable as fragrant hedges.

ABOVE *A rose trellis forms the backdrop to this beautiful display of lavender and allium.*

Lavender is one of the most familiar and popular of all scented plants.

CREATING A SCENTED ROSE GARDEN

ragrant roses are often considered to be the epitome of scented plants, combining an outstanding variety of beautiful flowers with a wide range of bouquets. Fragrances in shrub roses are described on pages 78–79, while climbing and rambling roses are detailed on pages 80–81. Their scents range from primrose, banana, and raspberry to myrrh, orange, and clove. Many Floribunda (cluster-flowered bush roses) and Hybrid Tea (large-flowered bush roses) are also fragrant and these are detailed here.

Roses create superb hedges, whether along a perimeter or within a garden, where they act as a decorative feature to separate one area from another. However, unlike evergreen hedges, which create privacy throughout the year, roses are deciduous and during winter are bare of leaves.

'Felicia' and 'Penelope' are two Hybrid Musks that are ideal for forming tall hedges. You must ensure that the plants of both are spaced about 30–36in (75–90cm) apart. The vigorous Floribunda 'The Queen Elizabeth' is another excellent choice.

For medium-sized hedges, several options exist. 'Céleste', a pretty Alba rose, has semidouble, sweetly scented, pink flowers with yellow stamens. 'Southampton' is a Floribunda rose with fragrant, apricot flowers. Space the plants 18in (45cm) apart.

RIGHT *'Madame Grégoire Staechelin' is an ideal pillar rose, or it can simply be allowed to swarm over a tree stump.*

PROJECT	ERECTING A PILLAR

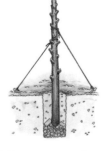

1 Preferably, choose a pole (usually from a conifer) that still has small shoots growing out of its sides. These help to give support to the rambler, especially in windy areas.

2 Dig a hole 3ft (90cm) deep and about 12in (30cm) square. Fill the base with clean rubble. This helps to keep the pole's base dry, especially during winter.

3 Place the pole in the hole and drop a few bricks around its base to hold it in the center of the hole. Use a level on two sides to check that the pole is vertical.

4 Use guy ropes or long pieces of wood to keep the pole upright. Alternatively, ask a friend to hold the pole. Then, add and firm soil around the base of the pole.

1 About four weeks before planting, thoroughly dig the soil; remove and compost perennial weeds and mix in some well-decomposed soil or manure.

2 The day before planting a container-grown rose, water the soil several times. Also, ensure that the soil in the planting area is moist but not waterlogged.

3 Dig out a hole, slightly deeper and wider than the container. When planting against a wall, leave a gap of 15in (38cm) between the brickwork and the plant.

4 Form the soil in the hole's base into a slight mound and firm it with your foot. Remove the container and position the soil-ball in the hole.

5 Use a straight-edged board to check that the soil-ball's surface is slightly below the surrounding soil. Firm friable soil around the soil-ball.

6 Insert a short bamboo cane to guide stems to the post or wall, and loosely secure the stems to it. Thoroughly water the soil and label the plant.

STAR PLANTS

A selection of shrub roses and climbing and rambling roses can be found on pages 79–81 of the plant directory. Listed here are the best of roses to use as scented features.

- Climbers
  R. 'Albéric Barbier'
  R. 'François Juranville'
  R. 'Madame Grégoire Staechelin'
  R. 'Veilchenblau'
  R. 'Zéphirine Drouhin'
- Shrub roses
  R. 'Buff Beauty'
  R. 'Fritz Nobis'
  R. 'Madame Hardy'
  R. 'Nymphenburg'
  R. 'Vanity'

If you are after a low hedge, 'White Pet', a bushy polyantha rose, has scented white flowers and grows about 18in (45cm) high. Space plants 12–15in (30–38cm) apart. 'The Fairy' is an excellent alternative. It bears slightly scented, rose-pink flowers on plants 18–24in (45–60cm) high. Space plants 15–18in (38–45cm) apart.

ERECTING A PILLAR

A pillar rose is ideal if you wish to grow a moderately vigorous climbing rose. Although you can use a tripod, it is easier to insert an 8–10ft- (2.4–3m-) long pole 30in (75cm) into the soil and plant a rambling rose close to it. A step-by-step guide to this process is featured opposite.

PLANTING A CLIMBING OR RAMBLING ROSE

Climbing and rambling roses need special care at planting time. Whereas soil in borders and beds is usually uniformly moist, that around pergola posts is often much drier, and especially at the base of a wall. Where this is the case, be sure to water thoroughly before planting.

Climbing and rambling roses are available from garden centers either growing in containers (for planting throughout the year whenever the soil is not frozen or the weather too cold) or "bare-rooted" (sold and planted in early spring, during their dormant period). The step-by-step sequence above provides easy-to-follow instructions on how to plant this kind of rose successfully.

CREATING A FRAGRANT HERB GARDEN

The range of herbs with aromatic leaves is wide; those such as thymes with an evergreen and perennial nature are described on page 103, while the many herbaceous mints are detailed on pages 97 and 98. Additionally, a wide range of annuals and biennials for herb gardens is featured on pages 92 and 93. Many herbs are small enough to be grown in windowboxes, troughs, and pots on a patio. Some, such as mints, have an invasive nature, and so constraining their roots in pots is an advantage.

Creating a cartwheel herb garden is an exciting and unusual way to grow herbs. It is especially suited to low-growing, leafy herbs that develop a sea of attractive foliage. During earlier years, these gardens were formed within old, perhaps partly broken, cartwheels. Nowadays, they can be inexpensively constructed by using large pebbles to represent the spokes, hub, and rim.

NOSEGAY GARDENS

A "nosegay" was originally a bunch of scented herbs which was held to the nose to mask the smell of public places when sanitation was poor. Nosegay gardens are richly scented borders close to patios or terraces. Some plant combinations can be grown in pots and tubs. Three good plants to consider for containers are chamomile, rosemary, and sweet bay. Chamomile (*Chamaemelum nobile*, earlier known as *Anthemis nobilis*) has leaves that have a delicately fruity fragrance when bruised. Rosemary (*Rosmarinus officinalis*) is an evergreen shrub that is ideal for planting alongside a path, with its foliage slightly intruding on to the paved area. It is also good for growing in a large tub. Plant five small plants (perhaps hardly more than rooted cuttings) in a tub 18–20in (45–50cm) wide, and pinch out growing tips to encourage bushiness. When plants become too large, trim lightly. Sweet bay (*Laurus nobilis*) is a distinctive evergreen, grown as a half-standard in a large pot or tub, and regularly clipped and pruned to a symmetrical shape. Its glossy green leaves emit a sweet fragrance.

| PROJECT | MAKING A CARTWHEEL HERB GARDEN |

 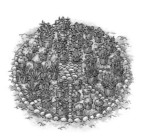  

1 During winter, dig an area of soil about 5ft (1.5m) square. Ensure the roots of perennial weeds are removed. Firm the soil by systematically shuffling sideways over the area, then tie a 2ft (60cm) long piece of string to two bamboo canes, place one in the center of the area, and draw a circle on the soil.

2 Use large pebbles to define the rim, then arrange pebbles to mark the positions of the spokes. Leave the herbs in their pots and place them in position to check that the planting areas are large enough. Use more pebbles to indicate the spokes and to form a hub about 9in (23cm) wide.

3 If the areas between the spokes are too large, they can be divided by adding a line of pebbles; small thymes will not need the same space as is required by large herbs such as sage and rosemary. To ensure that the surface is quickly covered by foliage, position small plants close together.

4 When the plants are in their final positions, remove their pots and use a trowel to plant them. Work outward from the center. Firm the soil around their roots, and then level the surface using the heel of your shoe. Gently water the plants and soil. To add to the attraction, spread colored gravel on the surface.

1 Water an overcrowded plant the day before. To remove the pot, place your fingers over the soil-ball and invert it. Tap its edge on a hard surface, so that the pot can be eased away from the soil-ball.

2 Carefully pull the plant into several separate pieces. Use only healthy and young parts from around the outside. Discard old and woody pieces from the plant's center.

3 Partly fill a small, clean pot with soil. Repot each piece to the same depth as before, leaving a gap of about ½in (12mm) between the pot's rim and the surface of the soil. Water the soil several times.

HERBS FOR ALL PLACES

There are many other places to plant herbs. Troughs and windowboxes make ideal homes for small, bushy herbs. Use attractive mints, marjoram, oregano, chives, and thymes. Growing-bags create homes for sages and mints. It is even possible to reuse growing-bags — perhaps those used during the previous year for tomatoes. Ornate pots, as well as those with cupped holes in their sides, are ideal for herbs on a patio. Parsley, thyme, and chives all create

LEFT *Herbs are such versatile plants that they can be used in the mixed border as well as in a dedicated herb bed.*

WATCHPOINTS

❧ Don't buy herbs that are pot-bound, with masses of roots growing out of the pot's base.

❧ Don't buy herbs that are very young, perhaps no more than cuttings. They will not have filled at least two-thirds of the soil with roots and therefore will be difficult to plant and establish.

❧ Check that herbs are not infested with pests and diseases. The plants will have suffered and you may introduce pests and diseases to other plants in your garden.

❧ Don't buy herbs with soil that is totally saturated with water; conversely, do not buy herbs that are planted in dry soil.

❧ Do not buy herbs that are unlabeled. A clearly printed label is an indication that a plant has been cared for.

memorable features. Even tiny gaps left between paving slabs on a patio provide homes for small, prostrate herbs such as thymes. On a grander scale, position paving slabs in a checkerboard pattern and plant larger plants, such as colored sages, in the gaps.

SCENTED WATER AND BOG GARDENS

*W*ater gardens can be equally as fragrant as shrub, herbaceous, or annual borders. Indeed, the natural vibrancy of water, with its ever-changing patterns of light, adds a further dimension to scented water lilies and other aquatic plants. Many marginal plants— those that nestle at the edge of a pond—are also fragrant. Boggy areas around informal and wildlife ponds also provide the opportunity for unusual fragrances, even though some, such as the fetid yellow skunk cabbage (Lysichiton americanus) and stinking Benjamin (Trillium erectum), are better appreciated by flies.

Several pond plants have distinctively fragrant flowers that help water gardens to become even more exciting. *Aponogeton distachyos* (water hawthorn) has white, deeply lobed flowers with black anthers, from June to October, that appear on stems above the water's surface and are surrounded by narrowly oval, light green leaves with maroon-brown markings. If you love water lilies, use the star plants box to find one to suit your garden.

MINIPONDS FOR A PATIO GARDEN

Miniature ponds on patios and terraces create attractive features throughout the summer. However, the water is likely to freeze during winter, so in early winter empty the pond and place the plants and fish in large containers in a greenhouse. For a quick guide to making an attractive minipond, follow the step-by-step sequence below.

Scented water lilies are the most flamboyant and showy of water plants. There is a good choice of water lilies for all ponds, whatever their size.

- For small ponds, plant dwarf species like *Nymphaea* 'Laydekeri Lilacea', which bears pale pink, cup-shaped flowers which darken with age.
- For slightly larger ponds, opt for *Nymphaea* 'Firecrest' or *N.* 'Odorata Sulphurea', which displays lightly scented canary-yellow, star-shaped flowers.
- For gardeners with large ponds, there are even more choices. *Nymphaea* 'Marliacea Albida' is a vigorous water lily with pure white flowers flushed pale pink on the back, while *N.* 'Rose Arey' has rose pink, star-shaped flowers with attractive yellow stamens.

PROJECT — **PLANTING A MINIPOND**

1 Fill a strong tub with water. If it is watertight, scrub it clean, empty the water, and place it in position. If the tub leaks slightly, leave it where it is for a few weeks to see if the wood expands to fill the gaps.

2 If the tub leaks profusely, place it in position and then line the inside with sturdy black plastic sheeting. Form pleats on the inside so that it looks neat.

3 Fill with clean water and use a pair of sharp scissors to trim off the surplus plastic sheeting level with the rim. Your tub is now ready for planting.

4 In early summer, buy healthy, well-established plants growing in plastic-mesh baskets. Follow the instructions opposite when planting water lilies; also ensure that other water plants are not initially totally submerged.

PLANTING A WATER LILY

1 Plastic-mesh baskets come in several sizes, from 4in (10cm) to 12in (30cm) wide, and shapes: most are square, some are round, while others are kidney-shaped. There are also louver-type planting baskets.

2 Select a basket to suit the vigor of the water lily and the shape of your pond. To prevent soil falling through the mesh, line the basket with coarse burlap. Ensure it completely covers the inside of the basket.

3 Fill the basket two-thirds full with clean, weed-free, heavy loam, enriched with a sprinkling of bonemeal to help the roots to become established. Proprietary soils are also available.

4 Unwrap the water lily and place it in a bucket of water for about a day to ensure that the roots are plump. Remove and allow excess water to drain. Form a hole in the soil, position the plant, and spread out the roots.

5 Cover and firm the soil over the roots. Ensure that the plant's crown is slightly deeper than before, with the soil's surface about 1½in (36mm) below the basket's rim. Then add a 1in (2.5cm) thick layer of clean sand.

6 Water the soil and place the basket in the water, so that the leaves float on the surface. To achieve this, place several bricks under the basket. As the stems and leaves grow, progressively remove the bricks to lower the plant.

LEFT *Miniponds are a stylish alternative to ponds and fountains, and can be used to grow a variety of plants.*

SCENTED BOG GARDENS

Fragrant plants introduce a further quality to bog gardens. Some of these have scented flowers, while others reveal their redolence when their stems or leaves are bruised. Their fragrances are wide ranging and include almond, camphor, cinnamon, tangerine, and vanilla. There are even real stinkers such as *Lysichiton americanus* (skunk cabbage) whose fetid aroma is irresistible to flies. Pages 106–107 of the plant directory contains a selection of bog plants in addition to marginal and aquatic perennial species. Try to include a variety of plants in your pond to create an attractive display over a long period.

CREATING A SCENTED ROCK GARDEN

The range of plants grown in rock gardens is wide, from true alpines to small perennials, bulbs, miniature shrubs, and dwarf conifers. They combine to create a delicate miniature landscape of flowers and foliage, and by choosing scented types a further dimension can be added. Scented rock garden plants can be used in many different ways.

Once you have decided that you want to grow rock plants in your garden, the next step is to decide how you want to show them off. Successful rock gardens require regular sunlight, should be free from falling leaves and other debris, and need a site that is free from perennial weeds.

Traditional rock gardens are created on a slight slope to show off the small plants. This should be facing the sun and away from overhanging trees. The soil needs to be well drained and free from weeds and soil pests.

Drystone walls are functional as well as decorative and can be used to create terraces on steep slopes. The wall should be sloped backward and filled behind with clean rubble to ensure water drains rapidly through weep-holes left every 4ft (1.2m) along the wall's base.

Raised beds introduce height to a garden. These resemble a continuous drystone wall, 2–3ft (60–90cm) high, formed around a mound of well-drained soil. A kidney-shaped raised bed looks attractive when positioned to one side of a lawn.

ABOVE *Troughs make ideal containers for alpines and other low-growing plants. Remember to add a layer of drainage material in the base of the trough before planting.*

PROJECT	CREATING A SCENTED TROUGH GARDEN

1 Thoroughly scrub a stone trough and position it on four strong house bricks. Make sure that it does not tilt, but position so that it slopes slightly toward the hole to ensure good drainage.

2 Place a piece of perforated gauze over the hole and line the base with broken clay pots or stones. Lay a thin layer of sharp sand over it and then half fill with soil, using a lime-free type if you have chosen lime-hating plants.

3 Place a couple of large rocks on the soil, and adjust their height so that the stones are half buried. Add more soil while putting in the plants. When complete, the soil's surface should be about 1in (2.5cm) below the rim to allow for ½in (12mm) of rock chippings and gravel, and enable plants to be watered adequately.

If you want to grow low growing, scented rock garden plants in an unusual way, plant them in cracks in a natural stone path. Be sure to position them where they cannot be trodden on.

Other ways to display rock plants include scented trough gardens and scree beds. Trough gardens are an ideal home for miniature bulbs, perennials, and aromatic miniature conifers. The easy-to-follow sequence opposite shows how to make a trough garden.

Scree beds are a natural-looking way to display a range of beautiful rock plants. In nature, a scree is an area of loose rock at the bottom of a cliff or gully. In a garden, a scree bed can be a feature on its own or at the base of a rock garden. Constructing a scree is detailed below.

STAR PLANTS

In addition to the rock garden plants featured on pages 74 and 75, the following are also excellent – and they are all described and illustrated in this book.

- *Allium moly*
- *Brachyscome iberidifolia*
- *Cyclamen hederifolium*
- *Daphne cneorum*
- *Dianthus chinensis* 'Frosted Mixed'
- *Limnanthes douglasii*
- *Myosotis alpestris*
- *Thymus x citriodorus*
- *Thymus herba-barona*
- *Thymus serpyllum*
- *Zaluzianskya capensis*

PROJECT | **CONSTRUCTING A SCREE BED**

1 Use a spade to dig out an area 15in (38cm) deep. Dump the subsoil but spread the topsoil on the surface of borders.

2 Spread a 6in (15cm) thick layer of clean rubble in the base, followed by a 2in (5cm) layer of coarse sand or gravel.

3 Lay a 6in (15cm) thick layer of compost formed of one part weed-free topsoil, one of moist peat, and three of sharp sand.

4 If the bed is next to a rock garden, position a few rocks so that they appear to be a small outcrop. This helps to unify the scree bed with the rock garden.

5 Plant rock garden plants; for each plant, carefully remove the pot and use a trowel to form a hole. Draw and firm the soil around the root ball.

6 When the bed has been planted, spread a 1in (2.5cm) thick layer of clean gravel or chippings over the entire area. Gently but thoroughly water the plants.

THE PLANT DIRECTORY

3

The spectrum of plants that have either scented flowers or aromatic leaves is incredibly wide and ranges from annuals and biennials to bulbs and corms, herbaceous perennials and other border plants, climbers, trees, and shrubs. Many of these plants are described and illustrated in the information-packed directory pages that follow.

LEFT *The evergreen shrub Daphne odora 'Aureomarginata' has pale purple sweet-scented flowers and glossy leaves that make it an attraction all the year round.*

HOW TO USE THIS DIRECTORY

The Plant Directory lists many of the plants that are featured in this book, together with a selection of other plants that are suitable for use in a scented garden. It is not intended to be exhaustive, and experienced gardeners will have their own favorites. However, this listing has been made with the specific requirements of a scented garden in mind, and will guide the beginner to a range of attractive and readily available flowering plants, shrubs, and trees with which to create a beautiful garden. Concise information on planting and maintaining the plants is given for each entry.

The Plant Directory is divided into different categories that group like plants together. Plants with scented flowers are grouped on pages 60 to 91 and plants with scented leaves appear on pages 92 to 107. The categories are annuals and biennials *(page 60)*, herbaceous and other border plants *(page 64)*, bulbs and corms *(page 70)*, rock plants *(page 74)*, climbers and shrubs for walls *(page 76)*, shrub roses *(page 78)*, climbing and rambling roses *(page 80)*, trees and shrubs *(page 82)*, scented herbs *(page 92)*, scented-leaved pelargoniums (geraniums) *(page 94)*, herbaceous and other border plants *(page 96)*, trees and shrubs *(page 100)*, aromatic conifers *(page 104)*, and water and bog garden plants *(page 106)*. The symbols panel accompanying each entry gives essential information on growing conditions.

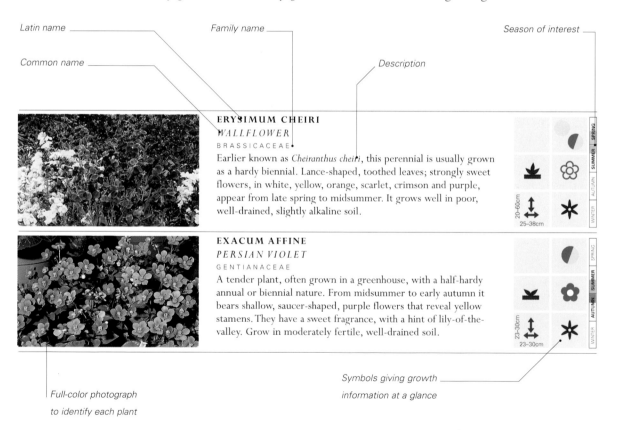

Latin name

Common name

Family name

Description

Season of interest

ERYSIMUM CHEIRI
WALLFLOWER
BRASSICACEAE
Earlier known as *Cheiranthus cheiri*, this perennial is usually grown as a hardy biennial. Lance-shaped, toothed leaves; strongly sweet flowers, in white, yellow, orange, scarlet, crimson and purple, appear from late spring to midsummer. It grows well in poor, well-drained, slightly alkaline soil.

20–60cm
25–38cm

EXACUM AFFINE
PERSIAN VIOLET
GENTIANACEAE
A tender plant, often grown in a greenhouse, with a half-hardy annual or biennial nature. From midsummer to early autumn it bears shallow, saucer-shaped, purple flowers that reveal yellow stamens. They have a sweet fragrance, with a hint of lily-of-the-valley. Grow in moderately fertile, well-drained soil.

23–30cm
23–30cm

Full-color photograph to identify each plant

Symbols giving growth information at a glance

KEY TO THE SYMBOLS

 EASY TO GROW

These are tolerant plants that require no special care or conditions in order to flourish.

 MODERATE TO GROW

These are plants that require some special care, such as protection from frost.

DIFFICULT TO GROW

These are plants that require a great deal of specialized care, and offer a challenge for the more experienced gardener.

 EVERGREEN

SEMIEVERGREEN

DECIDUOUS

Deciduous plants lose all their leaves in autumn (sometimes in summer), while evergreen plants keep their foliage all year. Plants described as semievergreen may keep some or all of their foliage through the winter in sheltered gardens or if the weather is mild. No leaf symbol is given for annuals, nor for biennials, although some biennials do keep their leaves over the first winter.

 FEATURE LEAVES

FEATURE SCENT

 FEATURE FLOWER

 **FEATURE FRUIT**

These symbols indicate the main feature of interest for each plant in the directory, but this is not necessarily the plant's only attractive asset. Some plants are given more than one symbol. This information will help you to choose plants that have complementary features, or plants that will perform a specific function in your garden.

 RAPID GROWTH

MODERATE GROWTH

SLOW GROWTH

Speed of growth is a highly subjective category, and will vary according to local conditions. Rapid growth indicates plants that reach their full extent in a single season, or plants that make substantial progress toward filling the space allowed for them in a single season. Slow growth indicates plants that take several seasons to reach their ultimate size. Moderate growth refers to rates of progress between these two extremes.

SEASON OF INTEREST

The period of the year when a plant is likely to be most attractive is also indicated (those plants that have something to offer all year round are marked accordingly). This will help you in creating a planting plan for each season.

HARDINESS ZONES

An indication of the frost-hardiness of each plant is given (a zone map can be found on page 112). In the case of annuals and tender perennials, you should check with your supplier to make sure you can offer the plant the right growing conditions.

 HEIGHT AND SPREAD

The size of plants will vary according to the growing conditions in your garden, so these measurements are a rough guide only. The measurements refer to the size of plants and trees when mature, although there are specific circumstances where the ultimate size is never reached.

 FULL SUN

PARTIAL SUN

SHADE

An indication of light preference is given to show each plant's optimum growing situation. Here again, this is only a rough guide, as some plants that prefer sun may also be reasonably tolerant of shade.

ANNUALS AND BIENNIALS

BRACHYSCOME IBERIDIFOLIA ●2–11

SWAN RIVER DAISY

ASTERACEAE

This hardy annual is invariably grown as a half-hardy annual in temperate areas, where it creates large, sweetly scented, daisylike flowers throughout summer in colors from white and pink to lilac and blue-purple. It requires well-drained but moisture-retentive, fertile soil and a warm position, sheltered from wind.

9–18in / 12–15in

CENTAUREA MOSCHATA ●2–11

SWEET SULTAN

ASTERACEAE

This popular annual is sometimes also known as *Amberboa moschata*. Its cornflowerlike flowers, each of which is about 3in (7.5cm) wide, come in white, pink, yellow, or purple, with a richly musklike fragrance. Grow it in a moderately fertile, well-drained soil.

18–24in / 10–12in

DATURA INOXIA ●6–9

INDIAN APPLE

SOLANACEAE

A half-hardy annual or tender perennial with a spreading nature and velvety, gray-green leaves. During mid- and late summer it develops 10–12in (25–30cm) long white trumpets tinged with pink. They open during the evenings. It thrives in fertile, well-drained soil.

24–36in / 3–4ft

DIANTHUS BARBATUS ●3–9

SWEET WILLIAM

CARYOPHYLLACEAE

This short-lived, bushy perennial is usually grown as a biennial. Light green to dark green leaves are joined by heads packed with sweetly scented flowers that smell slightly of cloves during late spring and early summer. Their colors range from white to red. Grow in fertile, well-drained, neutral to slightly alkaline soil.

12–24in / 10–15in

DIANTHUS CHINENSIS 'FROSTED MIXED' ●2–11

INDIAN PINK

CARYOPHYLLACEAE

A hardy annual, sometimes known as *Dianthus heddewigii* 'Frosted Mixed', with sweetly fragrant, double, and heavily laced flowers in two or three distinct colors. It is ideal for the edges of paths and borders. Grow it in light, well-drained, neutral to slightly alkaline soil.

12–15in / 8–10in

ERYSIMUM X ALLIONII ●2–9

SIBERIAN WALLFLOWER

BRASSICACEAE

This hardy perennial, earlier known as *Cheiranthus x allionii*, is invariably grown as a biennial. Lance-shaped, toothed leaves are joined by terminal spikes of sweetly scented flowers in spring; colors include orange, deep orange, and orange-gold. It likes poor, well-drained, slightly alkaline soil.

15in / 10–12in

≣ leaf type   ● light preference   ♨ speed of growth   ⚙ ease of growth

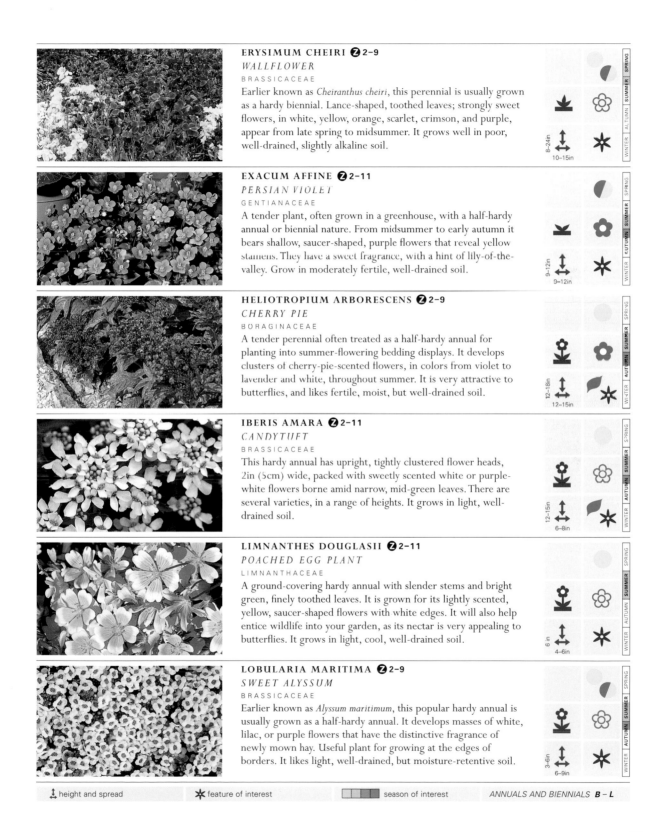

ERYSIMUM CHEIRI ❷ 2–9
WALLFLOWER
BRASSICACEAE

Earlier known as *Cheiranthus cheiri*, this perennial is usually grown as a hardy biennial. Lance-shaped, toothed leaves; strongly sweet flowers, in white, yellow, orange, scarlet, crimson, and purple, appear from late spring to midsummer. It grows well in poor, well-drained, slightly alkaline soil.

8–24in
10–15in

EXACUM AFFINE ❷ 2–11
PERSIAN VIOLET
GENTIANACEAE

A tender plant, often grown in a greenhouse, with a half-hardy annual or biennial nature. From midsummer to early autumn it bears shallow, saucer-shaped, purple flowers that reveal yellow stamens. They have a sweet fragrance, with a hint of lily-of-the-valley. Grow in moderately fertile, well-drained soil.

9–12in
9–12in

HELIOTROPIUM ARBORESCENS ❷ 2–9
CHERRY PIE
BORAGINACEAE

A tender perennial often treated as a half-hardy annual for planting into summer-flowering bedding displays. It develops clusters of cherry-pie-scented flowers, in colors from violet to lavender and white, throughout summer. It is very attractive to butterflies, and likes fertile, moist, but well-drained soil.

12–18in
12–15in

IBERIS AMARA ❷ 2–11
CANDYTUFT
BRASSICACEAE

This hardy annual has upright, tightly clustered flower heads, 2in (5cm) wide, packed with sweetly scented white or purple-white flowers borne amid narrow, mid-green leaves. There are several varieties, in a range of heights. It grows in light, well-drained soil.

12–15in
6–8in

LIMNANTHES DOUGLASII ❷ 2–11
POACHED EGG PLANT
LIMNANTHACEAE

A ground-covering hardy annual with slender stems and bright green, finely toothed leaves. It is grown for its lightly scented, yellow, saucer-shaped flowers with white edges. It will also help entice wildlife into your garden, as its nectar is very appealing to butterflies. It grows in light, cool, well-drained soil.

6 in
4–6in

LOBULARIA MARITIMA ❷ 2–9
SWEET ALYSSUM
BRASSICACEAE

Earlier known as *Alyssum maritimum*, this popular hardy annual is usually grown as a half-hardy annual. It develops masses of white, lilac, or purple flowers that have the distinctive fragrance of newly mown hay. Useful plant for growing at the edges of borders. It likes light, well-drained, but moisture-retentive soil.

3–6in
6–9in

⬍ height and spread   ✳ feature of interest   ▭ season of interest   *ANNUALS AND BIENNIALS* **B – L**

ANNUALS AND BIENNIALS

MALCOLMIA MARITIMA ⓩ 2–11
VIRGINIAN STOCK
BRASSICACEAE

A sweetly scented hardy annual with white, cross-shaped flowers that appear among blunt-tipped, gray-green leaves. Grows rapidly and flowers four weeks after sowing, then continues for six to eight weeks. Tolerant of salt spray, so an ideal choice for coastal gardens. It thrives in moderately fertile, well-drained soil.

6–8in
4–6in

MATTHIOLA BICORNIS ⓩ 2–11
NIGHT-SCENTED STOCK
BRASSICACEAE

An erect to spreading hardy annual grown, as its name suggests, for the strong fragrance it exudes after dusk. Its narrow, gray-green leaves are complemented by clusters of pink, purple, or mauve flowers in summer. It thrives in moderately fertile, moist but well-drained, preferably slightly alkaline soil.

15in
6–7in

MATTHIOLA INCANA ⓩ 3–8
GILLYFLOWER, STOCK
BRASSICACEAE

A half-hardy, erect annual with gray-green leaves and open spires of pink and white flowers that have a superb clovelike fragrance. Ideal for planting under windows or in beds alongside paths. Grow in a sheltered position and choose soil that is moderately fertile, well drained, and neutral to slightly alkaline.

12in
10in

MIRABILIS JALAPA ⓩ 2–5
FOUR O'CLOCK PLANT
NYCTAGINACEAE

A tender perennial usually grown as a half-hardy annual. This bushy plant has oval leaves and trumpet-shaped flowers in a wide range of colors and with a sweet, fruity fragrance. The flowers can have a short lifespan—opening in the afternoon and expiring by the next morning. Grow in a fertile, well-drained soil.

24in
12–15in

MYOSOTIS ALPESTRIS ⓩ 2–11
FORGET-ME-NOT
BORAGINACEAE

A bushy hardy perennial, invariably raised as a hardy biennial, with a diminutive nature that makes it ideal for planting in a rock garden. From late spring to early summer it bears fragrant, azure-blue flowers. Grow in fertile, moisture-retentive soil.

4–8in
6–8in

NICOTIANA ALATA ⓩ 2–9
FLOWERING TOBACCO PLANT
SOLANACEAE

A popular half-hardy annual, earlier known as *Nicotiana affinis*, with spoon-shaped leaves and clusters of tubular, 3in (7.5cm) long, very sweet flowers in a wide range of colors. It is ideal for evening fragrance. Grow in fertile, moist but well-drained soil. Taller plants will require staking.

18–30in
12–15in

leaf type	light preference	speed of growth	ease of growth

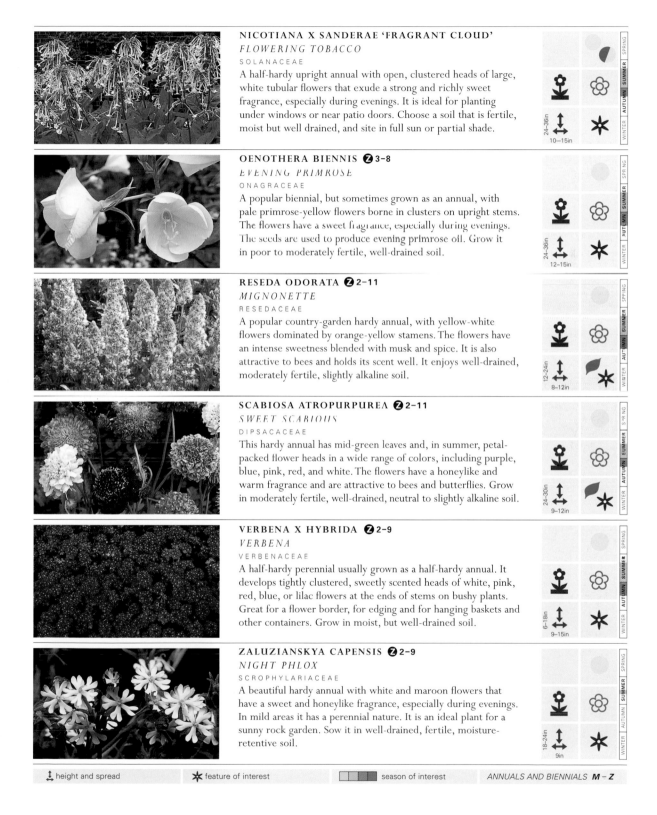

NICOTIANA X SANDERAE 'FRAGRANT CLOUD'
FLOWERING TOBACCO
SOLANACEAE

A half-hardy upright annual with open, clustered heads of large, white tubular flowers that exude a strong and richly sweet fragrance, especially during evenings. It is ideal for planting under windows or near patio doors. Choose a soil that is fertile, moist but well drained, and site in full sun or partial shade.

OENOTHERA BIENNIS ❷ 3–8
EVENING PRIMROSE
ONAGRACEAE

A popular biennial, but sometimes grown as an annual, with pale primrose-yellow flowers borne in clusters on upright stems. The flowers have a sweet fragrance, especially during evenings. The seeds are used to produce evening primrose oil. Grow it in poor to moderately fertile, well-drained soil.

RESEDA ODORATA ❷ 2–11
MIGNONETTE
RESEDACEAE

A popular country-garden hardy annual, with yellow-white flowers dominated by orange-yellow stamens. The flowers have an intense sweetness blended with musk and spice. It is also attractive to bees and holds its scent well. It enjoys well-drained, moderately fertile, slightly alkaline soil.

SCABIOSA ATROPURPUREA ❷ 2–11
SWEET SCABIOUS
DIPSACACEAE

This hardy annual has mid-green leaves and, in summer, petal-packed flower heads in a wide range of colors, including purple, blue, pink, red, and white. The flowers have a honeylike and warm fragrance and are attractive to bees and butterflies. Grow in moderately fertile, well-drained, neutral to slightly alkaline soil.

VERBENA X HYBRIDA ❷ 2–9
VERBENA
VERBENACEAE

A half-hardy perennial usually grown as a half-hardy annual. It develops tightly clustered, sweetly scented heads of white, pink, red, blue, or lilac flowers at the ends of stems on bushy plants. Great for a flower border, for edging and for hanging baskets and other containers. Grow in moist, but well-drained soil.

ZALUZIANSKYA CAPENSIS ❷ 2–9
NIGHT PHLOX
SCROPHYLARIACEAE

A beautiful hardy annual with white and maroon flowers that have a sweet and honeylike fragrance, especially during evenings. In mild areas it has a perennial nature. It is an ideal plant for a sunny rock garden. Sow it in well-drained, fertile, moisture-retentive soil.

↕ height and spread   ✳ feature of interest   ▭▭▭ season of interest   *ANNUALS AND BIENNIALS **M – Z***

HERBACEOUS PERENNIALS

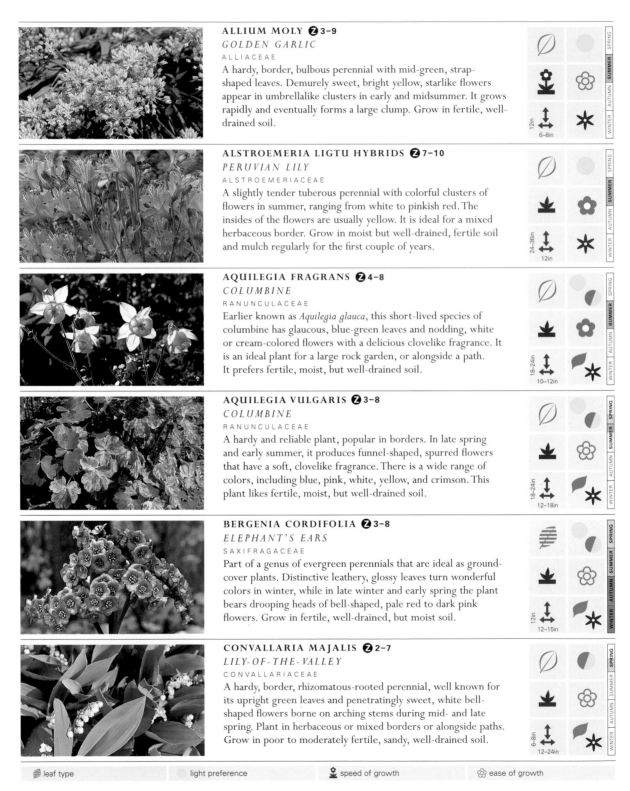

ALLIUM MOLY ❷ 3–9
GOLDEN GARLIC
ALLIACEAE

A hardy, border, bulbous perennial with mid-green, strap-shaped leaves. Demurely sweet, bright yellow, starlike flowers appear in umbrellalike clusters in early and midsummer. It grows rapidly and eventually forms a large clump. Grow in fertile, well-drained soil.

ALSTROEMERIA LIGTU HYBRIDS ❷ 7–10
PERUVIAN LILY
ALSTROEMERIACEAE

A slightly tender tuberous perennial with colorful clusters of flowers in summer, ranging from white to pinkish red. The insides of the flowers are usually yellow. It is ideal for a mixed herbaceous border. Grow in moist but well-drained, fertile soil and mulch regularly for the first couple of years.

AQUILEGIA FRAGRANS ❷ 4–8
COLUMBINE
RANUNCULACEAE

Earlier known as *Aquilegia glauca*, this short-lived species of columbine has glaucous, blue-green leaves and nodding, white or cream-colored flowers with a delicious clovelike fragrance. It is an ideal plant for a large rock garden, or alongside a path. It prefers fertile, moist, but well-drained soil.

AQUILEGIA VULGARIS ❷ 3–8
COLUMBINE
RANUNCULACEAE

A hardy and reliable plant, popular in borders. In late spring and early summer, it produces funnel-shaped, spurred flowers that have a soft, clovelike fragrance. There is a wide range of colors, including blue, pink, white, yellow, and crimson. This plant likes fertile, moist, but well-drained soil.

BERGENIA CORDIFOLIA ❷ 3–8
ELEPHANT'S EARS
SAXIFRAGACEAE

Part of a genus of evergreen perennials that are ideal as ground-cover plants. Distinctive leathery, glossy leaves turn wonderful colors in winter, while in late winter and early spring the plant bears drooping heads of bell-shaped, pale red to dark pink flowers. Grow in fertile, well-drained, but moist soil.

CONVALLARIA MAJALIS ❷ 2–7
LILY-OF-THE-VALLEY
CONVALLARIACEAE

A hardy, border, rhizomatous-rooted perennial, well known for its upright green leaves and penetratingly sweet, white bell-shaped flowers borne on arching stems during mid- and late spring. Plant in herbaceous or mixed borders or alongside paths. Grow in poor to moderately fertile, sandy, well-drained soil.

≡ leaf type   ● light preference   ⚘ speed of growth   ✿ ease of growth

DIANTHUS CARYOPHYLLUS ❷ 7–10
WILD CARNATION
CARYOPHYLLACEAE

This tufted perennial has bright gray-green leaves and during midsummer bears loose clusters of highly fragrant, single, bright or dull reddish-purple flowers. Like all *Dianthus*, it prefers to grow in well-drained, neutral to slightly alkaline soil and to be situated in direct sunlight.

DIANTHUS 'MRS SINKINS' ❷ 2–9
OLD-FASHIONED PINK
CARYOPHYLLACEAE

An old-fashioned variety that produces wonderful, double white flowers. It is often grown for its powerful scent and used to add splashes of color to borders. It is also very well known as a cut flower. It prefers well-drained, neutral to slightly alkaline soil in direct sunlight.

DICTAMNUS ALBUS ❷ 3–8
BURNING BUSH
RUTACEAE

This clump-forming herbaceous perennial is prized for its leathery, lemon-scented leaves and white to pinkish, spiderlike flowers borne in spires. The plant emits a heavy fragrance, while the old flower heads produce a volatile oil that can be burned during warm evenings. It likes most soils. Can cause a rash when touched.

FILIPENDULA CAMTSCHATICA ❷ 3–9
ROSACEAE

Also known as *Filipendula kamtschatica*, this herbaceous perennial has mid-green leaves, slightly hairy underneath. It develops large, open plumes of fleecy white flowers from mid- to late summer on branched stems. The flower plumes are 6–8in (15–20cm) wide and have a sweet and lingering fragrance. Plant it in moist, but well-drained, moderately fertile soil.

FILIPENDULA ULMARIA ❷ 3–9
MEADOWSWEET
ROSACEAE

A popular border plant with a wealth of dark green, coarsely serrated leaves. The exceptionally sweet, almond-scented, creamy-white flowers are borne in flattened heads, up to 6in (15cm) wide, throughout summer. Plant it in moderately fertile, moist soil.

GLADIOLUS CALLIANTHUS 'MURIELIAE' ❷ 8–10
PEACOCK ORCHID
IRIDACEAE

Still widely known as *Acidanthera bicolor* 'Murieliae', this slightly tender cormous perennial has upright, swordlike leaves and star-shaped white flowers with purple centers and a sweet fragrance. An ideal choice for a border, this plant does well in fertile, well-drained soil in full sun.

⬍ height and spread   ✳ feature of interest   ▭▭▭ season of interest   *HERBACEOUS PERENNIALS* **A – G**

HERBACEOUS PERENNIALS

GLADIOLUS TRISTIS CONCOLOR ❷7–10
EVENING FLOWER GLADIOLUS
IRIDACEAE

A superb border gladioli, this plant is also suitable for a large rock garden. It develops spikes of carnation-scented cream or pale yellow flowers, sometimes tinged green, during late spring and early summer. The upright and tapering leaves are dark green. Grow in fertile, well-drained soil.

15–18in
4–6in

SPRING · SUMMER · AUTUMN · WINTER

HEDYSARUM CORONARIUM ❷4–9
FRENCH HONEYSUCKLE
PAPILIONACEAE

This short-lived shrubby perennial can also be grown as a biennial or annual. Tiered flowers, with a bouquet reminiscent of clover, are borne in 3in (7.5cm) long spikes during late summer and early autumn. It is ideal as a cut flower. Grow in well-drained, stony or sandy, poor to fertile soil.

36–48in
18–24in

SPRING · SUMMER · AUTUMN · WINTER

HEMEROCALLIS CITRINA ❷3–10
DAYLILY
HEMEROCALLIDACEAE

A herbaceous perennial with arching, straplike leaves. Star-shaped, lemon-yellow flowers have a pronounced honeysucklelike fragrance during mid- and late summer. Originally from China, this plant requires a soil that is fertile, moist, but well drained and in full sun or light shade.

36–40in
24–30in

SPRING · SUMMER · AUTUMN · WINTER

HEMEROCALLIS 'HYPERION' ❷3–10
DAYLILY
HEMEROCALLIDACEAE

This superb border plant has narrow leaves and almost star-shaped, fragrant yellow flowers in midsummer. It is excellent for planting in a mixed or herbaceous border or possibly in a wildflower garden. Select a site with soil that is fertile, moist, but well drained.

30in
18in

SPRING · SUMMER · AUTUMN · WINTER

HEMEROCALLIS LILIOASPHODELUS ❷3–10
DAYLILY
HEMEROCALLIDACEAE

Earlier known as *Hemerocallis flava*, this hardy, herbaceous, clump-forming border plant bears masses of golden-yellow, trumpet-shaped flowers that exude the rich and penetrating sweetness of honeysuckle. It needs light, moisture-retentive, but well-drained soil.

30–36in
15–18in

SPRING · SUMMER · AUTUMN · WINTER

HESPERIS MATRONALIS ❷4–9
DAME'S VIOLET
BRASSICACEAE

This short-lived perennial, superb in a country garden, has dark green leaves and tall, pyramidal spikes of white, mauve, or purple, cross-shaped flowers during early and midsummer. They emit a sweet, clovelike fragrance, especially in the evenings. It thrives in light, moisture-retentive, but well-drained soil.

24–36in
15–18in

SPRING · SUMMER · AUTUMN · WINTER

≋ leaf type   ● light preference   ⚑ speed of growth   ⊗ ease of growth

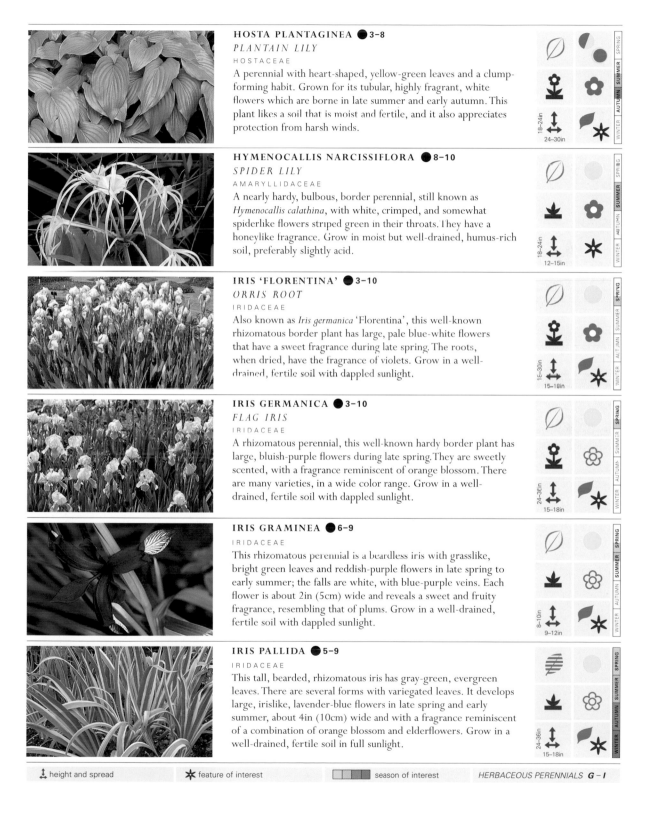

HOSTA PLANTAGINEA ●3–8
PLANTAIN LILY

HOSTACEAE

A perennial with heart-shaped, yellow-green leaves and a clump-forming habit. Grown for its tubular, highly fragrant, white flowers which are borne in late summer and early autumn. This plant likes a soil that is moist and fertile, and it also appreciates protection from harsh winds.

18–24in
24–30in

HYMENOCALLIS NARCISSIFLORA ●8–10
SPIDER LILY

AMARYLLIDACEAE

A nearly hardy, bulbous, border perennial, still known as *Hymenocallis calathina*, with white, crimped, and somewhat spiderlike flowers striped green in their throats. They have a honeylike fragrance. Grow in moist but well-drained, humus-rich soil, preferably slightly acid.

18–24in
12–15in

IRIS 'FLORENTINA' ●3–10
ORRIS ROOT

IRIDACEAE

Also known as *Iris germanica* 'Florentina', this well-known rhizomatous border plant has large, pale blue-white flowers that have a sweet fragrance during late spring. The roots, when dried, have the fragrance of violets. Grow in a well-drained, fertile soil with dappled sunlight.

18–30in
15–18in

IRIS GERMANICA ●3–10
FLAG IRIS

IRIDACEAE

A rhizomatous perennial, this well-known hardy border plant has large, bluish-purple flowers during late spring. They are sweetly scented, with a fragrance reminiscent of orange blossom. There are many varieties, in a wide color range. Grow in a well-drained, fertile soil with dappled sunlight.

24–36in
15–18in

IRIS GRAMINEA ●6–9

IRIDACEAE

This rhizomatous perennial is a beardless iris with grasslike, bright green leaves and reddish-purple flowers in late spring to early summer; the falls are white, with blue-purple veins. Each flower is about 2in (5cm) wide and reveals a sweet and fruity fragrance, resembling that of plums. Grow in a well-drained, fertile soil with dappled sunlight.

8–10in
9–12in

IRIS PALLIDA ●5–9

IRIDACEAE

This tall, bearded, rhizomatous iris has gray-green, evergreen leaves. There are several forms with variegated leaves. It develops large, irislike, lavender-blue flowers in late spring and early summer, about 4in (10cm) wide and with a fragrance reminiscent of a combination of orange blossom and elderflowers. Grow in a well-drained, fertile soil in full sunlight.

24–36in
15–18in

| ⇕ height and spread | ✳ feature of interest | ▭▭▭ season of interest | *HERBACEOUS PERENNIALS* **G – I** |

HERBACEOUS PERENNIALS

OENOTHERA MACROCARPA ⓩ 5–8
EVENING PRIMROSE
ONAGRACEAE
Formerly known as *Oenothera missouriensis*, this low-growing border or rock garden plant has mid-green, lance-shaped leaves, and red-spotted buds that open in the evening to reveal sweetly scented yellow flowers, up to 3in (7.5cm) wide. The best soil for this plant is poor to moderately fertile and well drained.

4–6in
15–18in

PAEONIA 'DUCHESSE DE NEMOURS' ⓩ 3–8
PEONY
PAEONIACEAE
This hardy herbaceous perennial has attractive green leaves and very large, fragrant, pure white, double flowers with spreading petals and a flush of green in bud, from late spring to midsummer. Grow in moist, but well-drained, deep, and fertile soil.

30–50in
24–30in

PAEONIA 'SARAH BERNHARDT' ⓩ 3–8
PEONY
PAEONIACEAE
This hardy herbaceous perennial, which is a hybrid of *Paeonia lactiflora*, is grown for its large, double, fragrant pink flowers, which have silver margins inside. They appear in early summer. It prefers to grow in moist, but well-drained, deep, and fertile soil.

30–40in
24–30in

PANCRATIUM MARITIMUM ⓩ 8–11
SEA DAFFODIL
AMARYLLIDACEAE
A slightly tender bulbous perennial, this border plant has long, narrow, straplike leaves and white, six-petaled flowers that are strongly sweet, with a slight hint of lilies. The leaves usually remain throughout winter in sheltered areas. It is good against a sunny wall. Grow in any well-drained soil in full sun.

12in
9in

PHLOX MACULATA ⓩ 5–8
MEADOW PHLOX, WILD SWEET WILLIAM
POLEMONIACEAE
A popular herbaceous perennial with upright stems bearing lance-shaped, mid-green leaves and tapering spires of purple flowers from midsummer to early autumn. There are also varieties in pink or white. These are strongly sweet-scented. Grow in fertile, moisture-retentive, but well-drained soil.

24–36in
15–18in

PHLOX PANICULATA ⓩ 4–8
SUMMER PHLOX, FALL PHLOX
POLEMONIACEAE
Also known as *Phlox decussata*, this hardy herbaceous perennial has upright stems and mid-green leaves. From midsummer to early autumn it has 4–6in (10–15cm) long clusters of sweetly scented purple flowers. There are several varieties, in a range of colors. Grow in a fertile, moisture-retentive, but well-drained soil.

18–40in
12–18in

SPRING | SUMMER | AUTUMN | WINTER

≣ leaf type   ● light preference   ⚲ speed of growth   ✿ ease of growth

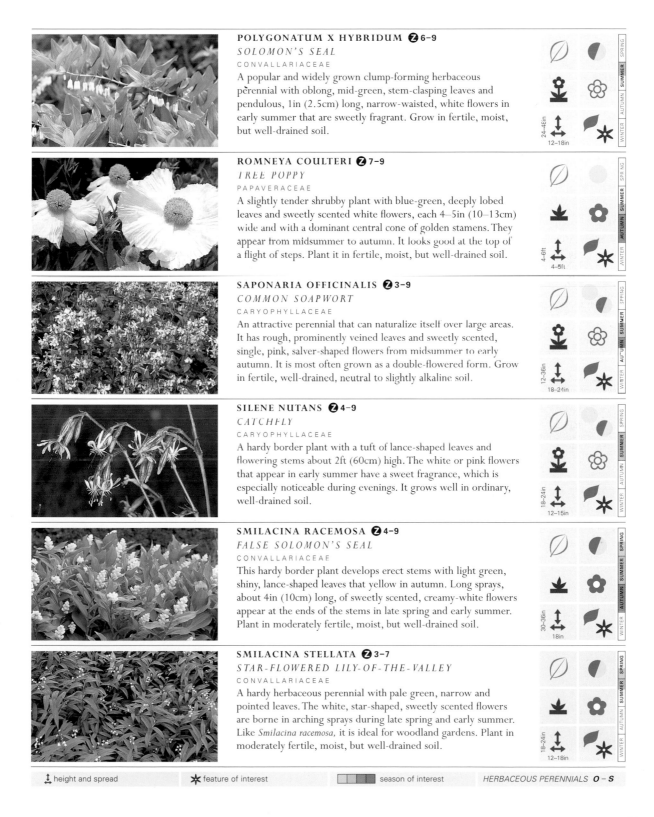

POLYGONATUM X HYBRIDUM ❷ 6–9
SOLOMON'S SEAL
CONVALLARIACEAE

A popular and widely grown clump-forming herbaceous perennial with oblong, mid-green, stem-clasping leaves and pendulous, 1in (2.5cm) long, narrow-waisted, white flowers in early summer that are sweetly fragrant. Grow in fertile, moist, but well-drained soil.

ROMNEYA COULTERI ❷ 7–9
TREE POPPY
PAPAVERACEAE

A slightly tender shrubby plant with blue-green, deeply lobed leaves and sweetly scented white flowers, each 4–5in (10–13cm) wide and with a dominant central cone of golden stamens. They appear from midsummer to autumn. It looks good at the top of a flight of steps. Plant it in fertile, moist, but well-drained soil.

SAPONARIA OFFICINALIS ❷ 3–9
COMMON SOAPWORT
CARYOPHYLLACEAE

An attractive perennial that can naturalize itself over large areas. It has rough, prominently veined leaves and sweetly scented, single, pink, salver-shaped flowers from midsummer to early autumn. It is most often grown as a double-flowered form. Grow in fertile, well-drained, neutral to slightly alkaline soil.

SILENE NUTANS ❷ 4–9
CATCHFLY
CARYOPHYLLACEAE

A hardy border plant with a tuft of lance-shaped leaves and flowering stems about 2ft (60cm) high. The white or pink flowers that appear in early summer have a sweet fragrance, which is especially noticeable during evenings. It grows well in ordinary, well-drained soil.

SMILACINA RACEMOSA ❷ 4–9
FALSE SOLOMON'S SEAL
CONVALLARIACEAE

This hardy border plant develops erect stems with light green, shiny, lance-shaped leaves that yellow in autumn. Long sprays, about 4in (10cm) long, of sweetly scented, creamy-white flowers appear at the ends of the stems in late spring and early summer. Plant in moderately fertile, moist, but well-drained soil.

SMILACINA STELLATA ❷ 3–7
STAR-FLOWERED LILY-OF-THE-VALLEY
CONVALLARIACEAE

A hardy herbaceous perennial with pale green, narrow and pointed leaves. The white, star-shaped, sweetly scented flowers are borne in arching sprays during late spring and early summer. Like *Smilacina racemosa,* it is ideal for woodland gardens. Plant in moderately fertile, moist, but well-drained soil.

⤢ height and spread   ✳ feature of interest   ▭▭▭ season of interest   *HERBACEOUS PERENNIALS* **O – S**

BULBS AND CORMS

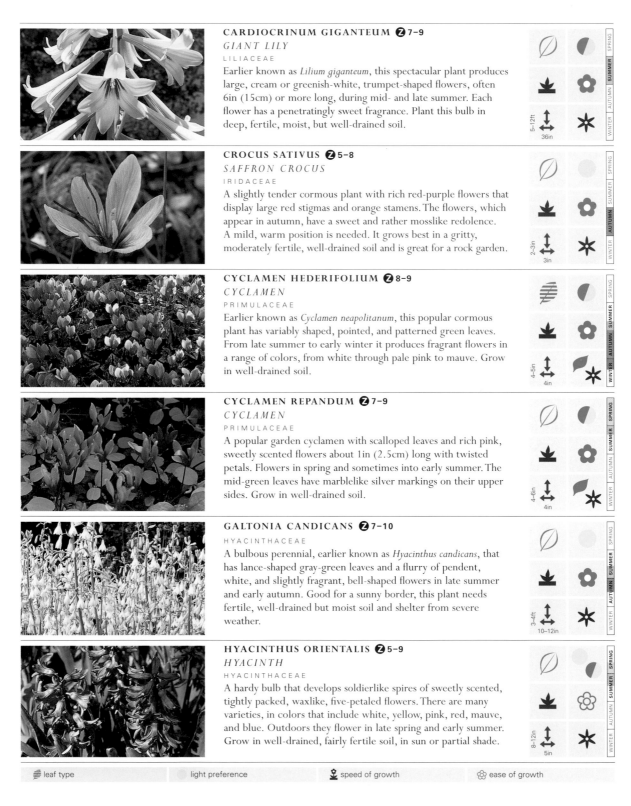

CARDIOCRINUM GIGANTEUM ❷7–9
GIANT LILY
LILIACEAE

Earlier known as *Lilium giganteum*, this spectacular plant produces large, cream or greenish-white, trumpet-shaped flowers, often 6in (15cm) or more long, during mid- and late summer. Each flower has a penetratingly sweet fragrance. Plant this bulb in deep, fertile, moist, but well-drained soil.

CROCUS SATIVUS ❷5–8
SAFFRON CROCUS
IRIDACEAE

A slightly tender cormous plant with rich red-purple flowers that display large red stigmas and orange stamens. The flowers, which appear in autumn, have a sweet and rather mosslike redolence. A mild, warm position is needed. It grows best in a gritty, moderately fertile, well-drained soil and is great for a rock garden.

CYCLAMEN HEDERIFOLIUM ❷8–9
CYCLAMEN
PRIMULACEAE

Earlier known as *Cyclamen neapolitanum*, this popular cormous plant has variably shaped, pointed, and patterned green leaves. From late summer to early winter it produces fragrant flowers in a range of colors, from white through pale pink to mauve. Grow in well-drained soil.

CYCLAMEN REPANDUM ❷7–9
CYCLAMEN
PRIMULACEAE

A popular garden cyclamen with scalloped leaves and rich pink, sweetly scented flowers about 1in (2.5cm) long with twisted petals. Flowers in spring and sometimes into early summer. The mid-green leaves have marblelike silver markings on their upper sides. Grow in well-drained soil.

GALTONIA CANDICANS ❷7–10
HYACINTHACEAE

A bulbous perennial, earlier known as *Hyacinthus candicans*, that has lance-shaped gray-green leaves and a flurry of pendent, white, and slightly fragrant, bell-shaped flowers in late summer and early autumn. Good for a sunny border, this plant needs fertile, well-drained but moist soil and shelter from severe weather.

HYACINTHUS ORIENTALIS ❷5–9
HYACINTH
HYACINTHACEAE

A hardy bulb that develops soldierlike spires of sweetly scented, tightly packed, waxlike, five-petaled flowers. There are many varieties, in colors that include white, yellow, pink, red, mauve, and blue. Outdoors they flower in late spring and early summer. Grow in well-drained, fairly fertile soil, in sun or partial shade.

≣ leaf type ● light preference ♟ speed of growth ✿ ease of growth

LEUCOJUM VERNUM ●4-8
SPRING SNOWFLAKE
AMARYLLIDACEAE

A hardy bulbous plant with long and arching, mid-green, straplike leaves and white, green-tipped, 3/4in (18mm) long flowers in early spring. They have a sweet scent. It is an ideal bulb for planting in a spring-flowering garden and requires soil that is moist, but well drained.

8–12in / 3in

MUSCARI ARMENIACUM ●4-8
GRAPE HYACINTH
HYACINTHACEAE

A hardy bulb with semierect leaves and stems tightly packed with deep blue, sweetly scented flowers with white rims. Several varieties, such as 'Heavenly Blue'(bright blue) and 'Cantab' (pale blue). Thrives in a soil that is fertile, moist, but well drained.

8in / 3in

NARCISSUS 'ACTEA' ●4-9
DAFFODIL
AMARYLLIDACEAE

An unusual daffodil that bears strongly fragrant flowers in late spring. These are open, rippled with a red ring surrounding the inner corona. Choose a site with moderately fertile, well-drained soil that will remain moist throughout the growing season.

18in / 4in

NARCISSUS JONQUILLA ●5-9
WILD JONQUIL
AMARYLLIDACEAE

This daffodil has erect but narrow leaves about 16–18in (40–45cm) long. It bears strongly scented, golden-yellow flowers with tiny flat cups in late spring. Originally from Spain, this plant does well in a site with moderately fertile, well-drained soil that will remain moist throughout the growing season.

12in / 4in

TULIPA SAXATILIS ●4-9
CANDIA TULIP
LILIACEAE

A hardy bulbous plant with bright, pinkish-lilac flowers with deep yellow centers that have a faintly primrose fragrance. One to three flowers are produced on each stem, and are borne amid shiny green leaves. Grow in soil that is fertile and well drained, and choose a site that is sheltered from harsh winds.

8–10in / 6in

TULIPA SYLVESTRIS ●4-9
TULIP
LILIACEAE

A hardy bulb with light-green, glaucous leaves and lightly sweet, freely produced, yellow flowers about 2in (5cm) long and with reflexed outer petals in mid- and late spring. The leaves are narrow and gray-green in color. Grow in soil that is fertile and well drained and choose a site that is sheltered from harsh winds.

14–16in / 4in

⬍ height and spread   ✳ feature of interest   ▭▭▭ season of interest   *BULBS AND CORMS* **C – T**

FRAGRANT LILIES

LILIUM AURATUM ●5–8
GOLDEN-RAYED LILY
LILIACEAE
Hardy, bulbous, stem-rooting lily with stiff stems and strongly sweet, funnel-shaped, brilliant white flowers during late summer and early autumn. They are up to 12in (30cm) wide, with golden bands or rays, and purple wine-colored spots on the inner surfaces. It likes well-drained, moisture-retentive, lime-free soil.

2–5ft / 10in

LILIUM 'BLACK DRAGON' ●4–8
LILY
LILIACEAE
This stem-rooting Olympic Hybrid has sweetly scented, trumpet-shaped, dark red flowers with white insides. Up to 12 flowers are borne on each stem, creating a magnificent display in mid- and late summer. It thrives in soil that is well drained and enriched with organic material. It is tolerant of lime in the soil.

5ft / 10in

LILIUM 'BRIGHT STAR' ●5–7
LILY
LILIACEAE
A lime-tolerant lily with large, outward-facing white flowers in mid- and late summer. Its spreading petals are curved at the tips and have an orange band, which creates a starlike effect. It likes soil that is well drained and enriched with leaf or other organic material.

3–5ft / 10in

LILIUM CANDIDUM ●6–9
MADONNA LILY
LILIACEAE
This hardy, basal-rooting bulb develops large, bell-shaped, pure white flowers about 3in (7.5cm) long during early and midsummer. Each flower has a mass of golden anthers at its center, and exudes a strong, honeylike fragrance. It likes soil that is moisture-retentive, but well drained and slightly alkaline.

3–6ft / 9in

LILIUM CHALCEDONICUM ●7–9
OLD SCARLET MARTAGON
LILIACEAE
A hardy, basal-rooting bulb with slightly sweet, pendulous, Turk's-caplike, brilliant scarlet flowers borne in large clusters during mid- and late summer. The flowers have a slightly orange fragrance when just opening. It is an ideal lily to create a dominant splash of color in borders. It likes well-drained soil.

2–5ft / 12in

LILIUM FORMOSIANUM ●7–9
LILY
LILIACEAE
A half-hardy, stem-rooting bulb with narrowly trumpet-shaped, white flowers about 6in (15cm) long during late summer and into early autumn. Sometimes the flowers are marked with chocolate or reddish-purple. It requires lime-free soil and full sun or partial shade.

2–5ft / 12–15in

≣ leaf type | ● light preference | ⚥ speed of growth | ⊛ ease of growth

LILIUM HANSONII ❷ 2–7
JAPANESE TURK'S-CAP LILY
LILIACEAE

A hardy, stem-rooting lily with small, sweetly scented, nodding, Turk's-caplike, pale orange-yellow flowers with purplish-brown spots during early and midsummer. Each flower has an attractive waxy sheen. It thrives in a soil that is well-drained, lime-free, and enriched with leaf mold.

3–5ft / 10in

LILIUM HENRYI ❷ 3–8
LILY
LILIACEAE

A tall and dominant, hardy, stem-rooting lily with arching stems that bear many pale orange-yellow flowers with red spots in late summer and early autumn. Each flower has a delicate but distinctive sweetness. Support the tall stems. It thrives in well-drained, but moisture-retentive soil.

3–10ft / 12in

LILIUM LONGIFLORUM ❷ 7–9
EASTER LILY
LILIACEAE

An excellent plant for a container, this is a slightly tender, stem-rooting bulb with trumpet-shaped, glistening white flowers with golden pollen during mid- and late summer. The 5–7in (13–18cm) wide flowers exude a heavy fragrance, reminiscent of jasmine. A lime-tolerant lily, it does well in most soils.

16–39in / 9in

LILIUM REGALE ❷ 4–7
ROYAL LILY, REGAL LILY
LILIACEAE

A hardy, stem-rooting lily with strongly sweet, white, funnel-shaped flowers up to 5in (13cm) wide during midsummer. They are borne in loose clusters and the center of each flower is sulfur-yellow; the backs are shaded rose-purple. Grow in most well-drained soils, apart from extremely alkaline ones.

2–6ft / 10in

LILIUM SPECIOSUM ❷ 4–8
JAPANESE LILY
LILIACEAE

Half-hardy, stem-rooting lily with sweetly scented, white, bowl-shaped flowers up to 3–5in (7.5–13cm) long appearing in late summer and early autumn. The recurved and wavy petals are heavily shaded with crimson. It is ideal for growing in pots. Grow in lime-free soil.

3–6ft / 12in

LILIUM X TESTACEUM ❷ 6–9
NANKEEN LILY
LILIACEAE

A hardy, basal-rooting bulb with pendulous, Turk's-caplike, apricot-yellow flowers during early and midsummer. They are sweetly scented and about 3in (7.5cm) long, with the interiors spotted red. The red anthers bear orange pollen. This lime-tolerant lily will do well in a well-drained, fertile soil.

3–5ft / 12in

↕ height and spread   ✳ feature of interest   ▭▭▭ season of interest   *FRAGRANT LILIES* **L – L**

ROCK PLANTS

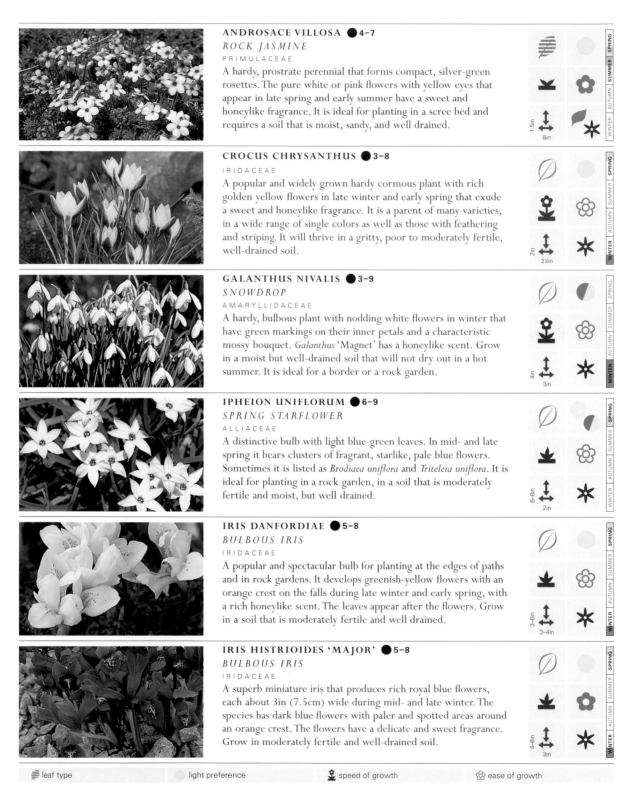

ANDROSACE VILLOSA ●4–7
ROCK JASMINE
PRIMULACEAE

A hardy, prostrate perennial that forms compact, silver-green rosettes. The pure white or pink flowers with yellow eyes that appear in late spring and early summer have a sweet and honeylike fragrance. It is ideal for planting in a scree bed and requires a soil that is moist, sandy, and well drained.

1.5in / 8in — SPRING SUMMER AUTUMN WINTER

CROCUS CHRYSANTHUS ●3–8
IRIDACEAE

A popular and widely grown hardy cormous plant with rich golden yellow flowers in late winter and early spring that exude a sweet and honeylike fragrance. It is a parent of many varieties, in a wide range of single colors as well as those with feathering and striping. It will thrive in a gritty, poor to moderately fertile, well-drained soil.

2in / 2½in — SPRING SUMMER AUTUMN WINTER

GALANTHUS NIVALIS ●3–9
SNOWDROP
AMARYLLIDACEAE

A hardy, bulbous plant with nodding white flowers in winter that have green markings on their inner petals and a characteristic mossy bouquet. *Galanthus* 'Magnet' has a honeylike scent. Grow in a moist but well-drained soil that will not dry out in a hot summer. It is ideal for a border or a rock garden.

4in / 3in — SPRING SUMMER AUTUMN WINTER

IPHEION UNIFLORUM ●6–9
SPRING STARFLOWER
ALLIACEAE

A distinctive bulb with light blue-green leaves. In mid- and late spring it bears clusters of fragrant, starlike, pale blue flowers. Sometimes it is listed as *Brodiaea uniflora* and *Triteleia uniflora*. It is ideal for planting in a rock garden, in a soil that is moderately fertile and moist, but well drained.

6–8in / 2in — SPRING SUMMER AUTUMN WINTER

IRIS DANFORDIAE ●5–8
BULBOUS IRIS
IRIDACEAE

A popular and spectacular bulb for planting at the edges of paths and in rock gardens. It develops greenish-yellow flowers with an orange crest on the falls during late winter and early spring, with a rich honeylike scent. The leaves appear after the flowers. Grow in a soil that is moderately fertile and well drained.

3–6in / 3–4in — SPRING SUMMER AUTUMN WINTER

IRIS HISTRIOIDES 'MAJOR' ●5–8
BULBOUS IRIS
IRIDACEAE

A superb miniature iris that produces rich royal blue flowers, each about 3in (7.5cm) wide during mid- and late winter. The species has dark blue flowers with paler and spotted areas around an orange crest. The flowers have a delicate and sweet fragrance. Grow in moderately fertile and well-drained soil.

4–6in / 3in — SPRING SUMMER AUTUMN WINTER

≣ leaf type   ● light preference   ⚘ speed of growth   ⚙ ease of growth

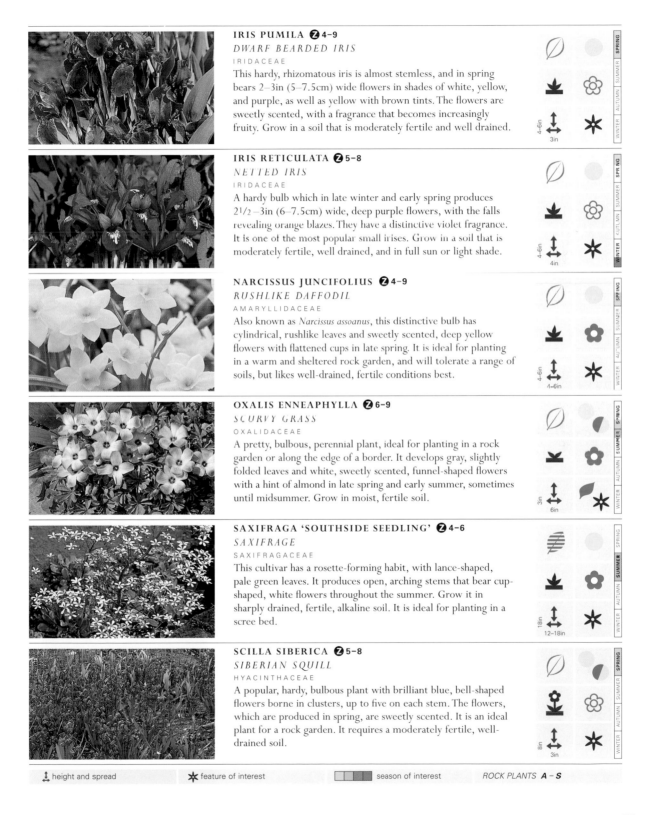

IRIS PUMILA ❷ 4–9

DWARF BEARDED IRIS

IRIDACEAE

This hardy, rhizomatous iris is almost stemless, and in spring bears 2–3in (5–7.5cm) wide flowers in shades of white, yellow, and purple, as well as yellow with brown tints. The flowers are sweetly scented, with a fragrance that becomes increasingly fruity. Grow in a soil that is moderately fertile and well drained.

IRIS RETICULATA ❷ 5–8

NETTED IRIS

IRIDACEAE

A hardy bulb which in late winter and early spring produces 2¹/₂–3in (6–7.5cm) wide, deep purple flowers, with the falls revealing orange blazes. They have a distinctive violet fragrance. It is one of the most popular small irises. Grow in a soil that is moderately fertile, well drained, and in full sun or light shade.

NARCISSUS JUNCIFOLIUS ❷ 4–9

RUSHLIKE DAFFODIL

AMARYLLIDACEAE

Also known as *Narcissus assoanus*, this distinctive bulb has cylindrical, rushlike leaves and sweetly scented, deep yellow flowers with flattened cups in late spring. It is ideal for planting in a warm and sheltered rock garden, and will tolerate a range of soils, but likes well-drained, fertile conditions best.

OXALIS ENNEAPHYLLA ❷ 6–9

SCURVY GRASS

OXALIDACEAE

A pretty, bulbous, perennial plant, ideal for planting in a rock garden or along the edge of a border. It develops gray, slightly folded leaves and white, sweetly scented, funnel-shaped flowers with a hint of almond in late spring and early summer, sometimes until midsummer. Grow in moist, fertile soil.

SAXIFRAGA 'SOUTHSIDE SEEDLING' ❷ 4–6

SAXIFRAGE

SAXIFRAGACEAE

This cultivar has a rosette-forming habit, with lance-shaped, pale green leaves. It produces open, arching stems that bear cup-shaped, white flowers throughout the summer. Grow it in sharply drained, fertile, alkaline soil. It is ideal for planting in a scree bed.

SCILLA SIBERICA ❷ 5–8

SIBERIAN SQUILL

HYACINTHACEAE

A popular, hardy, bulbous plant with brilliant blue, bell-shaped flowers borne in clusters, up to five on each stem. The flowers, which are produced in spring, are sweetly scented. It is an ideal plant for a rock garden. It requires a moderately fertile, well-drained soil.

⇕ height and spread   ✳ feature of interest   ▮▮▮▮ season of interest   *ROCK PLANTS* **A – S**

CLIMBERS AND WALL SHRUBS

AKEBIA QUINATA ⓩ 5–9
CHOCOLATE VINE
LARDIZABALACEAE

A twining, semievergreen climber with leaves formed of five leaflets. The dark chocolate-purple, pendent flowers, which appear in late spring, have a sweet vanilla scent; it is also claimed to be rather spicy, with a pervasive nature. Grow in a moist, but well-drained, fertile soil.

30+ft / 12–15ft

CLEMATIS FLAMMULA ⓩ 7–9
FRAGRANT VIRGIN'S BOWER
RANUNCULACEAE

This scrambling deciduous or semievergreen climber creates a mass of white flowers in large, open clusters from late summer to mid-autumn. They have a sweet and hawthornlike fragrance. It develops attractive seed heads. Plant where the roots are shaded and in a soil that is fertile and well drained.

20ft / 3ft

CLEMATIS MONTANA ⓩ 6–9
MOUNTAIN CLEMATIS
RANUNCULACEAE

A vigorous and well-known deciduous climber with pure white, sweetly scented, 2in (5cm) wide flowers borne in large clusters for about four weeks in late spring and early summer. There are several varieties, in a range of colors including pink. Plant it where the roots are shaded, in a soil that is fertile and well drained.

15–45ft / 6–10ft

CLEMATIS REHDERIANA ⓩ 6–9
RANUNCULACEAE

A vigorous deciduous climber with small, nodding, bell-shaped, primrose-yellow flowers from midsummer to early autumn, which reveal a delicate and slightly sweet fragrance with a hint of cowslips. The pendent flowers are borne in erect clusters that are up to 6–9in (15–23cm) long. Plant in soil that is fertile and well drained.

20–22ft / 6–10ft

CYTISUS BATTANDIERI ⓩ 7–9
PINEAPPLE BROOM
PAPILIONACEAE

In cold regions this deciduous shrub is best grown against a wall. It bears large, silvery leaves, but it is best known for its golden-yellow, pineapple-scented flowers borne in 4in (10cm) long clusters in late spring and early summer. Grow in soil that is moderately fertile and well drained.

15ft / 15ft

JASMINUM OFFICINALE ⓩ 6–9
JASMINE
OLEACEAE

A vigorous, twining, and popular deciduous climber that develops large, open clusters of pure white flowers from early summer to mid-autumn. These have the scent of jasmine and a rich sweetness. They are borne amid mid-green leaves. Grow in fertile, well-drained soil against a wall or other suitable support.

10ft / 10ft

≣ leaf type   light preference   ♨ speed of growth   ⚙ ease of growth

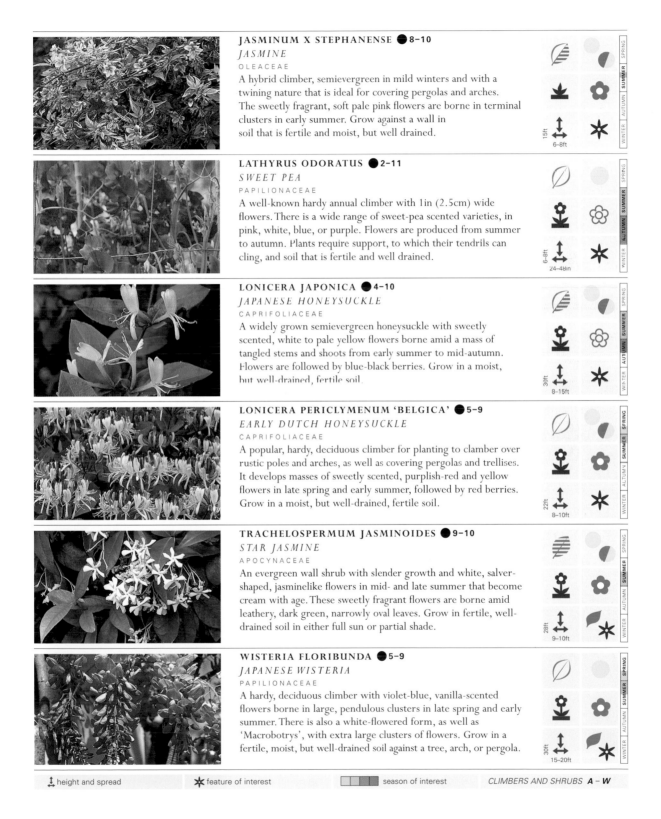

JASMINUM X STEPHANENSE ●8–10
JASMINE
OLEACEAE

A hybrid climber, semievergreen in mild winters and with a twining nature that is ideal for covering pergolas and arches. The sweetly fragrant, soft pale pink flowers are borne in terminal clusters in early summer. Grow against a wall in soil that is fertile and moist, but well drained.

15ft / 6–8ft

LATHYRUS ODORATUS ●2–11
SWEET PEA
PAPILIONACEAE

A well-known hardy annual climber with 1in (2.5cm) wide flowers. There is a wide range of sweet-pea scented varieties, in pink, white, blue, or purple. Flowers are produced from summer to autumn. Plants require support, to which their tendrils can cling, and soil that is fertile and well drained.

6–8ft / 24–48in

LONICERA JAPONICA ●4–10
JAPANESE HONEYSUCKLE
CAPRIFOLIACEAE

A widely grown semievergreen honeysuckle with sweetly scented, white to pale yellow flowers borne amid a mass of tangled stems and shoots from early summer to mid-autumn. Flowers are followed by blue-black berries. Grow in a moist, but well-drained, fertile soil.

30ft / 8–15ft

LONICERA PERICLYMENUM 'BELGICA' ●5–9
EARLY DUTCH HONEYSUCKLE
CAPRIFOLIACEAE

A popular, hardy, deciduous climber for planting to clamber over rustic poles and arches, as well as covering pergolas and trellises. It develops masses of sweetly scented, purplish-red and yellow flowers in late spring and early summer, followed by red berries. Grow in a moist, but well-drained, fertile soil.

22ft / 8–10ft

TRACHELOSPERMUM JASMINOIDES ●9–10
STAR JASMINE
APOCYNACEAE

An evergreen wall shrub with slender growth and white, salver-shaped, jasminelike flowers in mid- and late summer that become cream with age. These sweetly fragrant flowers are borne amid leathery, dark green, narrowly oval leaves. Grow in fertile, well-drained soil in either full sun or partial shade.

28ft / 9–10ft

WISTERIA FLORIBUNDA ●5–9
JAPANESE WISTERIA
PAPILIONACEAE

A hardy, deciduous climber with violet-blue, vanilla-scented flowers borne in large, pendulous clusters in late spring and early summer. There is also a white-flowered form, as well as 'Macrobotrys', with extra large clusters of flowers. Grow in a fertile, moist, but well-drained soil against a tree, arch, or pergola.

30ft / 15–20ft

↕ height and spread   ✳ feature of interest   ▭▭▭ season of interest   *CLIMBERS AND SHRUBS* **A – W**

SHRUB ROSES

ROSA 'ABRAHAM DARBY' **Z** 5–9
ROSE
ROSACEAE

A superb shrub, this New English rose has large, deeply cupped blooms in shades of yellow and apricot during early summer, and with repeat flowering. They have a rich, fruitlike fragrance and are produced over a long period. The plant is bushy and resistant to disease. Thrives in fertile, moist, well-drained soil.

5ft × 5ft

ROSA 'BUFF BEAUTY' **Z** 6–9
ROSE
ROSACEAE

During early summer and again later, this Hybrid Musk has large trusses of medium-size, petal-packed, warm apricot-yellow flowers with a bouquet of freshly opened packets of tea, combined with a slightly tarry scent. These are borne amid dark green leaves. It prefers fertile, moist, well-drained soil.

5ft × 5ft

ROSA 'CERISE BOUQUET' **Z** 5–9
ROSE
ROSACEAE

An exceptionally beautiful Modern Shrub rose with large, open sprays of semidouble, cerise-pink flowers borne on strong, arching stems during early summer, and small, gray leaves. The flowers have a distinctive raspberrylike fragrance. It thrives in fertile, moist, but well-drained soil.

10ft × 10ft

ROSA 'CHIANTI' **Z** 5–10
ROSE
ROSACEAE

A popular New English rose with large, freely produced, cup-shaped, deep crimson flowers during early and midsummer. With age, the flowers become a glorious purplish-maroon. These have a strongly Old Rose fragrance. It thrives in fertile, moist, but well-drained soil.

5–8ft × 5–8ft

ROSA 'CORNELIA' **Z** 6–9
ROSE
ROSACEAE

A superb Hybrid Musk, often grown as a hedge, with double, very fragrant, coppery-apricot flowers that change to coppery-pink. Flowers first appear in early summer and intermittently until autumn. They are borne in large trusses. It likes fertile, moist, but well-drained soil.

5ft × 5ft

ROSA 'DUPONTII' **Z** 4–9
ROSE
ROSACEAE

A nearly thornless, beautiful shrub with gray-green leaves and masses of blush-white, cream-tinted flowers in midsummer, with the rich aroma of bananas. They are borne singly or in clusters along arching stems, and are followed by orange-colored hips (fruits). Plant it in fertile, moist, well-drained soil.

7ft × 7ft

≣ leaf type | ● light preference | 🌶 speed of growth | ✿ ease of growth

ROSA 'FRITZ NOBIS' ❷5–9
ROSE
ROSACEAE

A superb Modern Shrub rose with attractively scrolled buds that are like those of Hybrid Tea roses, while its midsummer flowers are a delicate fresh pink with darker shading and the fragrance of cloves. The flowers are followed by reddish hips (fruits). It thrives in fertile, moist, but well-drained soil.

4–5ft / 4–5ft

ROSA 'HERITAGE' ❷5–9
ROSE
ROSACEAE

A superb New English rose, with medium-size, cupped, clear shell-pink flowers during early summer, and again later. The fragrance is exquisite, having overtones of lemon combined with the scent of an Old Rose. It is also suitable for planting as a climber. It thrives in fertile, moist, well-drained soil.

4ft / 4ft

ROSA 'MADAME HARDY' ❷4–9
ROSE
ROSACEAE

A beautiful Damask rose with medium-size, full-petaled, cupped, white flowers in midsummer that exude a delightful lemonlike fragrance. It is a vigorous shrub, packed with prickles and thorns. It likes fertile, moist, but well-drained soil.

5ft / 5ft

ROSA 'NYMPHENBURG' ❷4–9
ROSE
ROSACEAE

A bold, dramatic, and floriferous Modern Shrub rose with strong, arching stems bearing large, fully double, warm salmon-pink flowers shaded cerise in early and midsummer. The whole flower has a sweet and green-applelike scent. It likes fertile, moist, but well-drained soil.

6–8ft / 4–6ft

ROSA 'THE COUNTRYMAN' ❷5–10
ROSE
ROSACEAE

A superb New English rose with an Old Rose appearance and fragrance. It has two main flushes of flowers, during early summer and later, with occasional blooms between. It bears clear rose-pink flowers which open flat to form a rosette. It likes fertile, moist, but well-drained soil.

3–4ft / 3–4ft

ROSA 'VANITY' ❷6–9
ROSE
ROSACEAE

An open and large Hybrid Musk with sprays of crimson buds throughout most of the summer that open to reveal large, single, clear pink flowers that emit the rich fragrance of sweet peas. It is a dominant shrub and requires plenty of space. Grow in fertile, moist, but well-drained soil.

6–8ft / 5–6ft

↕ height and spread   ✳ feature of interest   ▭ season of interest   *SHRUB ROSES* **A – V**

CLIMBING AND RAMBLING ROSES

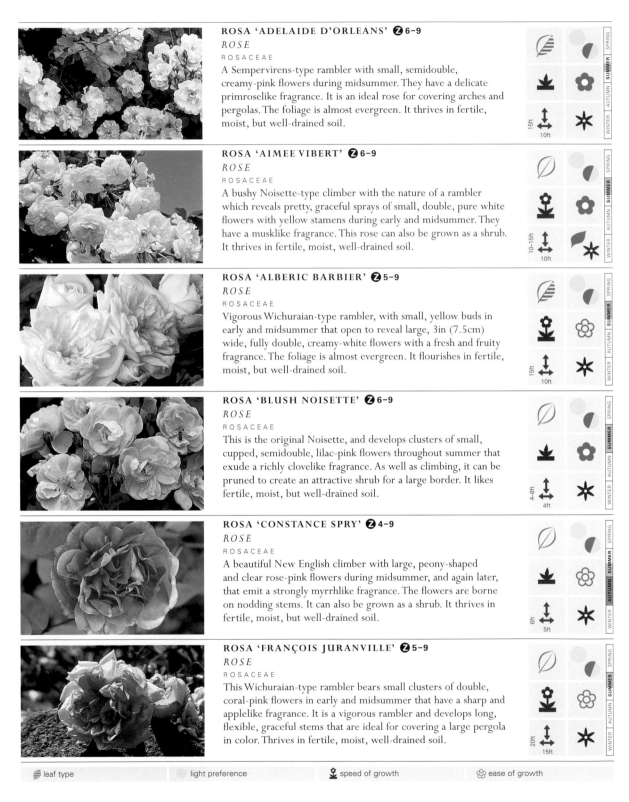

ROSA 'ADELAIDE D'ORLEANS' ❷ 6–9
ROSE
ROSACEAE

A Sempervirens-type rambler with small, semidouble, creamy-pink flowers during midsummer. They have a delicate primroselike fragrance. It is an ideal rose for covering arches and pergolas. The foliage is almost evergreen. It thrives in fertile, moist, but well-drained soil.

ROSA 'AIMEE VIBERT' ❷ 6–9
ROSE
ROSACEAE

A bushy Noisette-type climber with the nature of a rambler which reveals pretty, graceful sprays of small, double, pure white flowers with yellow stamens during early and midsummer. They have a musklike fragrance. This rose can also be grown as a shrub. It thrives in fertile, moist, well-drained soil.

ROSA 'ALBERIC BARBIER' ❷ 5–9
ROSE
ROSACEAE

Vigorous Wichuraian-type rambler, with small, yellow buds in early and midsummer that open to reveal large, 3in (7.5cm) wide, fully double, creamy-white flowers with a fresh and fruity fragrance. The foliage is almost evergreen. It flourishes in fertile, moist, but well-drained soil.

ROSA 'BLUSH NOISETTE' ❷ 6–9
ROSE
ROSACEAE

This is the original Noisette, and develops clusters of small, cupped, semidouble, lilac-pink flowers throughout summer that exude a richly clovelike fragrance. As well as climbing, it can be pruned to create an attractive shrub for a large border. It likes fertile, moist, but well-drained soil.

ROSA 'CONSTANCE SPRY' ❷ 4–9
ROSE
ROSACEAE

A beautiful New English climber with large, peony-shaped and clear rose-pink flowers during midsummer, and again later, that emit a strongly myrrhlike fragrance. The flowers are borne on nodding stems. It can also be grown as a shrub. It thrives in fertile, moist, but well-drained soil.

ROSA 'FRANÇOIS JURANVILLE' ❷ 5–9
ROSE
ROSACEAE

This Wichuraian-type rambler bears small clusters of double, coral-pink flowers in early and midsummer that have a sharp and applelike fragrance. It is a vigorous rambler and develops long, flexible, graceful stems that are ideal for covering a large pergola in color. Thrives in fertile, moist, well-drained soil.

≣ leaf type   ● light preference   ⚲ speed of growth   ⚙ ease of growth

ROSA 'GERBE ROSE' ❷ 5–9
ROSE

ROSACEAE

A Wichuraian-type rambler with large clusters of double, quartered, pink flowers during midsummer, and again later. They are tinted with cream and borne on rather stiff stems, and have a deliciously peonylike fragrance. It is an ideal rose for planting as a pillar rose. Thrives in fertile, moist, well-drained soil.

ROSA 'LEVERKUSEN' ❷ 5–9
ROSE

ROSACEAE

Hardy and reliable Kordessi-type climber, with rosette-shaped, lemon-yellow flowers during midsummer, and again later, with a distinctive lemon fragrance. It is ideal for covering a wall, as a pillar rose, or as a large shrub. It thrives in fertile, moist, but well-drained soil.

ROSA 'MADAME GREGOIRE STAECHELIN' ❷ 5–9
ROSE

ROSACEAE

A popular climber with long, shapely buds that open to reveal semidouble, glossy coral-pink flowers in early summer that are overlaid and splashed with crimson. These flowers have a delicate sweet pea fragrance and hang in large clusters. Thrives in fertile, moist, but well-drained soil.

ROSA 'THE GARLAND' ❷ 5–9
ROSE

ROSACEAE

A beautiful old rambler with spectacular bunches of small, semidouble, white to blush flowers with a rich orange scent during midsummer. It can also be grown as a large shrub. Additionally it bears small red hips (fruits). It likes fertile, moist, well-drained soil.

ROSA 'VEILCHENBLÀU' ❷ 5–9
ROSE

ROSACEAE

A distinctive Multiflora-type rambler with massed bunches of small, dark magenta, semidouble flowers in midsummer that fade to lilac and are sometimes streaked with white. They have a rich orange fragrance. It is ideal for training as a pillar rose. Thrives in fertile, moist, but well-drained soil.

ROSA 'ZEPHIRINE DROUHIN' ❷ 6–9
ROSE

ROSACEAE

A well-known Bourbon-type climber with masses of deep, rose-pink flowers during early summer, and again later. They have a sweet and penetrating fragrance, with a slight raspberrylike bouquet. It is an ideal climber for planting against a shady, cold wall. Thrives in fertile, moist, but well-drained soil.

⇕ height and spread   ✴ feature of interest   ▢▢▢▢ season of interest   *CLIMBING ROSES* **A – Z**

TREES AND SHRUBS

ABELIOPHYLLUM DISTICHUM ⓩ 5–9
WHITE FORSYTHIA
OLEACEAE
This slightly tender and slow-growing deciduous shrub has dull, dark green leaves that frequently turn purple in autumn. It bears small, star-shaped white or pink flowers in late winter or early spring. It is a good plant for training against a wall. Grow in fertile, well-drained soil.

5ft / 5ft

AZALEAS—DECIDUOUS TYPES ⓩ 3–9
ERICACEAE
Properly known as rhododendrons, these sweetly scented, floriferous, deciduous shrubs are in a wide range of colors, from white through yellow and pink to red. Flowering is during late spring and early summer. They have a range of heights and spreads; their leaves often assume rich tints in autumn. Grow in moist but well-drained, fertile, acid soil, in a sheltered site.

4–8ft / 3–7ft

AZARA MICROPHYLLA ⓩ 8–10
FLACOURTIACEAE
This tender. evergreen wall shrub, which in warm regions forms a small tree, bears pairs of small, dark, glossy green, dainty leaves. It creates dense clusters of small, yellow, strongly vanilla-scented flowers during late winter and spring. A warm, sunny wall is essential for this plant. Grow in moist, fertile soil.

30ft / 12ft

BUDDLEJA ALTERNIFOLIA ⓩ 6–9
BUDDLEJACEAE
Earlier known as *Buddleia alternifolia*, this deciduous shrub or small tree has narrow, lance-shaped, pale green leaves. The small, lavender-blue flowers are borne in rounded clusters on arching branches in early summer. They have a sweet fragrance, with a slight bouquet of heliotrope. Grow in fertile, well-drained soil. It makes an ideal specimen plant.

12ft / 12ft

BUDDLEJA DAVIDII ⓩ 6–9
BUTTERFLY BUSH
BUDDLEJACEAE
Earlier known as *Buddleia davidii*, from midsummer until autumn this deciduous shrub develops long, tapering, plumelike spires packed with lilac-purple flowers that are sweetly scented and with a hint of honey and musk. It is irresistible to butterflies and there are several varieties. Grow in fertile, well-drained soil.

10ft / 15ft

BUDDLEJA FALLOWIANA ⓩ 8–9
BUDDLEJACEAE
This slightly tender, deciduous shrub has a bushy nature and gray, lance-shaped leaves with silvery undersides and arching stems. Small, pale lavender-blue, sweetly scented flowers are borne in terminal, plumelike clusters, each up to 10in (25cm) long, from midsummer to early autumn. It is attractive to insects. Grow in fertile, well-drained soil.

6ft / 10ft

≣ leaf type	● light preference	⚓ speed of growth	⚙ ease of growth

BUDDLEJA GLOBOSA ❷ 7–9

ORANGE-BALL TREE

BUDDLEJACEAE

Earlier known as *Buddleia globosa*, this is a slightly tender evergreen shrub; in cold areas it becomes semievergreen. In early summer, it has clusters of orange-yellow flowers, like small tangerines, that have a sweet and honeylike fragrance. Grow in fertile, well-drained soil.

CALYCANTHUS FLORIDUS ❷ 5–9

CAROLINA ALLSPICE

CALYCANTHACEAE

A deciduous shrub with aromatic, dark green leaves and 2in (5cm) wide, reddish-purple flowers tinged brown in early and midsummer. They have the fragrance of ripe apples and strawberries, while the leaves, wood, and roots smell of camphor. The bark has a cinnamon fragrance. Grow in moist, fertile soil.

CEANOTHUS 'GLOIRE DE VERSAILLES' ❷ 7–10

CALIFORNIAN LILAC

RHAMNACEAE

A deciduous shrub with an open nature and long stems that bear 8in (20cm) long spires of soft powder-blue flowers from midsummer to autumn. They have a demurely sweet fragrance. In warm countries, where there is little risk of frost, it tends to have a dense nature. It likes fertile and well-drained soil.

CHIMONANTHUS PRAECOX ❷ 7–9

WINTERSWEET

CALYCANTHACEAE

This bushy, twiggy, deciduous shrub, earlier known as *Chimonanthus fragrans*, has lance-shaped, glossy green leaves and develops cup-shaped, clawlike flowers with ivory-colored petals and purple centers in winter. They reveal a heavy and spicy fragrance, with hints of violets and jonquils. Grow in a fertile, well-drained soil.

CLERODENDRUM CHINENSE 'PLENIFLORUM' ❷ 9–10

GLORY BOWER

VERBENACEAE

Earlier known as *Clerodendrum philippinum*, this tender deciduous subshrub has sparsely toothed green leaves and clusters of double pink or white flowers, sometimes tinged blue during mid- and late summer. They have a sweet and clove-scented fragrance. Grow in fertile, moist, but well-drained soil.

CLERODENDRUM TRICHOTOMUM ❷ 7–9

VERBENACEAE

A bushy, slow-growing deciduous shrub with large leaves and star-shaped, pinkish-white flowers borne in heads up to 9in (23cm) wide from midsummer to early autumn. They are sweetly scented, with a hint of jasmine. The leaves have an unpleasant fetid aroma when bruised. Grow in fertile, moist, but well-drained soil.

⬍ height and spread   ✳ feature of interest   ▮▮▮ season of interest   *TREES AND SHRUBS* **A – C**

TREES AND SHRUBS

CLETHRA ALNIFOLIA ❷ 3–9
SWEET PEPPER BUSH
CLETHRACEAE

An erect and bushy deciduous shrub with mid-green, pear-shaped to oblong leaves. The bell-shaped, creamy white, richly spicy flowers with undertones of cloves are borne in upright clusters up to 6in (15cm) long in late summer and early autumn. Grow in acid, moist, but well-drained fertile soil.

8ft / 8ft

CORONILLA VALENTINA GLAUCA ❷ 8–9
PAPILIONACEAE

This slightly tender, evergreen, spreading shrub has bluish-green, glaucous leaves formed of many leaflets. The bright yellow flowers are produced from late spring to midsummer in clusters of ten to fourteen. They have the unusual and rich, sweet fragrance of ripe plums. Site in light, well-drained, and moderately fertile soil.

5ft / 5ft

CORYLOPSIS PAUCIFLORA ❷ 6–9
BUTTERCUP WINTER HAZEL
HAMAMELIDACEAE

A densely branched, twiggy, deciduous shrub with bright green leaves and bell-shaped, pale primrose-yellow flowers in early and mid-spring borne in drooping clusters from bare stems. They are sweetly scented, with a hint of cowslips. Grow in fertile, moist, but well-drained acid soil.

5ft / 8ft

CYTISUS 'PORLOCK' ❷ 6–9
BROOM
PAPILIONACEAE

A beautiful half-hardy semievergreen shrub with an upright nature and sweetly scented, pea-shaped, butter-yellow flowers borne in clusters at the ends of young stems in mid- and late spring. It is best planted in the shelter of a wall. Site in well-drained, moderately fertile soil.

10ft / 10ft

CYTISUS X PRAECOX ❷ 6–9
BROOM
PAPILIONACEAE

This bushy, deciduous shrub creates a mass of long, slender, arching stems that in mid- and late spring bear pea-shaped, creamy-white flowers that emit a heavy and acrid scent. There are several varieties; 'Albus' is white, while 'Allgold' has sulfur-yellow flowers. Site in well-drained, moderately fertile soil.

4ft / 5ft

DAPHNE BLAGAYANA ❷ 7–9
THYMELAEACEAE

A low-growing, ground-hugging, evergreen shrub with creamy-white, deliciously scented flowers borne in clustered, upward-facing heads in spring. These are followed by fleshy white or pink fruit. The whole plant has a sprawling, somewhat sparse, and straggly nature; it creates an attractively informal feature. Grow in moderately fertile, well-drained soil.

16in / 3ft

🍃 leaf type   ◐ light preference   ⚘ speed of growth   ✿ ease of growth

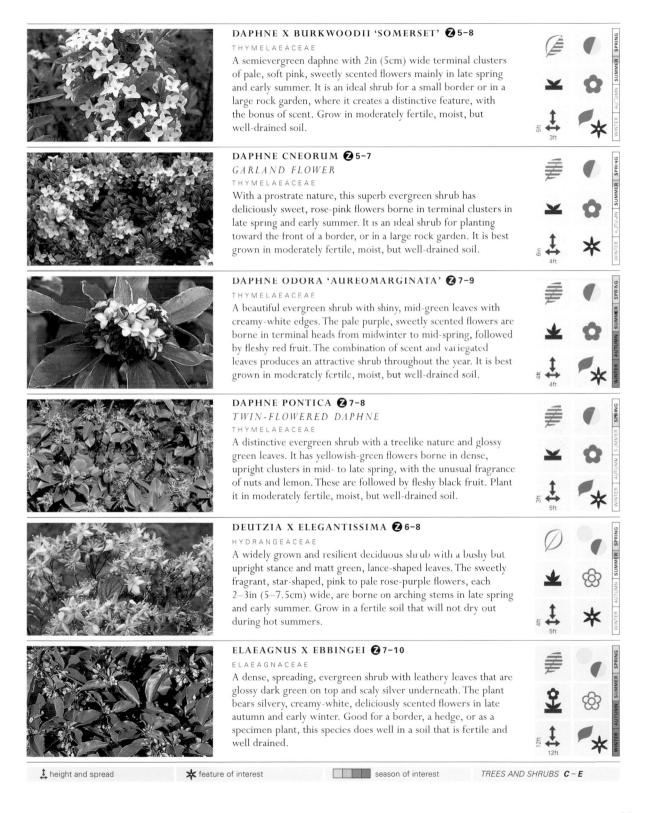

DAPHNE X BURKWOODII 'SOMERSET' **Z** 5–8
THYMELAEACEAE

A semievergreen daphne with 2in (5cm) wide terminal clusters of pale, soft pink, sweetly scented flowers mainly in late spring and early summer. It is an ideal shrub for a small border or in a large rock garden, where it creates a distinctive feature, with the bonus of scent. Grow in moderately fertile, moist, but well-drained soil.

5ft / 3ft

DAPHNE CNEORUM **Z** 5–7
GARLAND FLOWER
THYMELAEACEAE

With a prostrate nature, this superb evergreen shrub has deliciously sweet, rose-pink flowers borne in terminal clusters in late spring and early summer. It is an ideal shrub for planting toward the front of a border, or in a large rock garden. It is best grown in moderately fertile, moist, but well-drained soil.

6in / 4ft

DAPHNE ODORA 'AUREOMARGINATA' **Z** 7–9
THYMELAEACEAE

A beautiful evergreen shrub with shiny, mid-green leaves with creamy-white edges. The pale purple, sweetly scented flowers are borne in terminal heads from midwinter to mid-spring, followed by fleshy red fruit. The combination of scent and variegated leaves produces an attractive shrub throughout the year. It is best grown in moderately fertile, moist, but well-drained soil.

4ft / 4ft

DAPHNE PONTICA **Z** 7–8
TWIN-FLOWERED DAPHNE
THYMELAEACEAE

A distinctive evergreen shrub with a treelike nature and glossy green leaves. It has yellowish-green flowers borne in dense, upright clusters in mid- to late spring, with the unusual fragrance of nuts and lemon. These are followed by fleshy black fruit. Plant it in moderately fertile, moist, but well-drained soil.

3ft / 5ft

DEUTZIA X ELEGANTISSIMA **Z** 6–8
HYDRANGEACEAE

A widely grown and resilient deciduous shrub with a bushy but upright stance and matt green, lance-shaped leaves. The sweetly fragrant, star-shaped, pink to pale rose-purple flowers, each 2–3in (5–7.5cm) wide, are borne on arching stems in late spring and early summer. Grow in a fertile soil that will not dry out during hot summers.

4ft / 5ft

ELAEAGNUS X EBBINGEI **Z** 7–10
ELAEAGNACEAE

A dense, spreading, evergreen shrub with leathery leaves that are glossy dark green on top and scaly silver underneath. The plant bears silvery, creamy-white, deliciously scented flowers in late autumn and early winter. Good for a border, a hedge, or as a specimen plant, this species does well in a soil that is fertile and well drained.

12ft / 12ft

↕ height and spread   ✳ feature of interest   ▭▭▭ season of interest   *TREES AND SHRUBS **C – E***

TREES AND SHRUBS

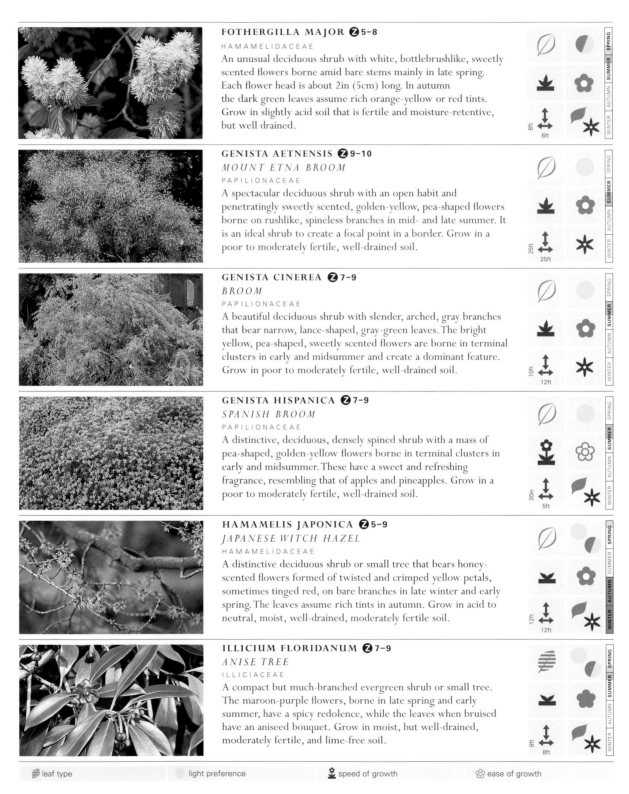

FOTHERGILLA MAJOR ⓩ 5–8

HAMAMELIDACEAE

An unusual deciduous shrub with white, bottlebrushlike, sweetly scented flowers borne amid bare stems mainly in late spring. Each flower head is about 2in (5cm) long. In autumn the dark green leaves assume rich orange-yellow or red tints. Grow in slightly acid soil that is fertile and moisture-retentive, but well drained.

GENISTA AETNENSIS ⓩ 9–10

MOUNT ETNA BROOM

PAPILIONACEAE

A spectacular deciduous shrub with an open habit and penetratingly sweetly scented, golden-yellow, pea-shaped flowers borne on rushlike, spineless branches in mid- and late summer. It is an ideal shrub to create a focal point in a border. Grow in a poor to moderately fertile, well-drained soil.

GENISTA CINEREA ⓩ 7–9

BROOM

PAPILIONACEAE

A beautiful deciduous shrub with slender, arched, gray branches that bear narrow, lance-shaped, gray-green leaves. The bright yellow, pea-shaped, sweetly scented flowers are borne in terminal clusters in early and midsummer and create a dominant feature. Grow in poor to moderately fertile, well-drained soil.

GENISTA HISPANICA ⓩ 7–9

SPANISH BROOM

PAPILIONACEAE

A distinctive, deciduous, densely spined shrub with a mass of pea-shaped, golden-yellow flowers borne in terminal clusters in early and midsummer. These have a sweet and refreshing fragrance, resembling that of apples and pineapples. Grow in a poor to moderately fertile, well-drained soil.

HAMAMELIS JAPONICA ⓩ 5–9

JAPANESE WITCH HAZEL

HAMAMELIDACEAE

A distinctive deciduous shrub or small tree that bears honey-scented flowers formed of twisted and crimped yellow petals, sometimes tinged red, on bare branches in late winter and early spring. The leaves assume rich tints in autumn. Grow in acid to neutral, moist, well-drained, moderately fertile soil.

ILLICIUM FLORIDANUM ⓩ 7–9

ANISE TREE

ILLICIACEAE

A compact but much-branched evergreen shrub or small tree. The maroon-purple flowers, borne in late spring and early summer, have a spicy redolence, while the leaves when bruised have an aniseed bouquet. Grow in moist, but well-drained, moderately fertile, and lime-free soil.

⊜ leaf type   ● light preference   ⚘ speed of growth   ⚙ ease of growth

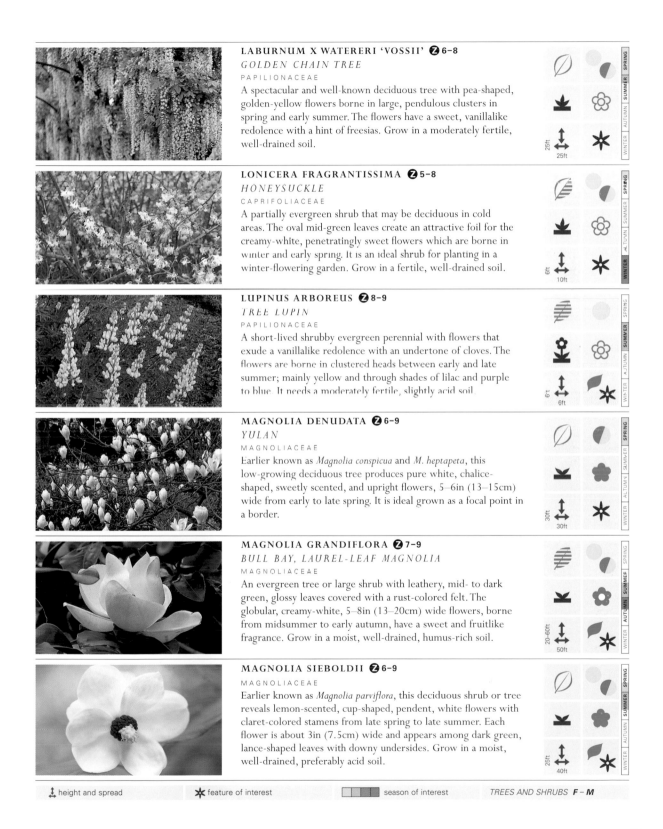

LABURNUM X WATERERI 'VOSSII' Z 6–8
GOLDEN CHAIN TREE
PAPILIONACEAE

A spectacular and well-known deciduous tree with pea-shaped, golden-yellow flowers borne in large, pendulous clusters in spring and early summer. The flowers have a sweet, vanillalike redolence with a hint of freesias. Grow in a moderately fertile, well-drained soil.

25ft / 25ft

LONICERA FRAGRANTISSIMA Z 5–8
HONEYSUCKLE
CAPRIFOLIACEAE

A partially evergreen shrub that may be deciduous in cold areas. The oval mid-green leaves create an attractive foil for the creamy-white, penetratingly sweet flowers which are borne in winter and early spring. It is an ideal shrub for planting in a winter-flowering garden. Grow in a fertile, well-drained soil.

6ft / 10ft

LUPINUS ARBOREUS Z 8–9
TREE LUPIN
PAPILIONACEAE

A short-lived shrubby evergreen perennial with flowers that exude a vanillalike redolence with an undertone of cloves. The flowers are borne in clustered heads between early and late summer; mainly yellow and through shades of lilac and purple to blue. It needs moderately fertile, slightly acid soil.

6ft / 6ft

MAGNOLIA DENUDATA Z 6–9
YULAN
MAGNOLIACEAE

Earlier known as *Magnolia conspicua* and *M. heptapeta*, this low-growing deciduous tree produces pure white, chalice-shaped, sweetly scented, and upright flowers, 5–6in (13–15cm) wide from early to late spring. It is ideal grown as a focal point in a border.

30ft / 30ft

MAGNOLIA GRANDIFLORA Z 7–9
BULL BAY, LAUREL-LEAF MAGNOLIA
MAGNOLIACEAE

An evergreen tree or large shrub with leathery, mid- to dark green, glossy leaves covered with a rust-colored felt. The globular, creamy-white, 5–8in (13–20cm) wide flowers, borne from midsummer to early autumn, have a sweet and fruitlike fragrance. Grow in a moist, well-drained, humus-rich soil.

20–60ft / 50ft

MAGNOLIA SIEBOLDII Z 6–9
MAGNOLIACEAE

Earlier known as *Magnolia parviflora*, this deciduous shrub or tree reveals lemon-scented, cup-shaped, pendent, white flowers with claret-colored stamens from late spring to late summer. Each flower is about 3in (7.5cm) wide and appears among dark green, lance-shaped leaves with downy undersides. Grow in a moist, well-drained, preferably acid soil.

25ft / 40ft

⸸ height and spread　　✳ feature of interest　　▭ season of interest　　*TREES AND SHRUBS* **F – M**

TREES AND SHRUBS

MAGNOLIA STELLATA **Z** 5–9
STAR MAGNOLIA
MAGNOLIACEAE

This widely grown deciduous shrub or tree develops star-shaped, white, sweetly fragrant flowers, 3–4in (7.5–10cm) wide in early and mid-spring before the leaves arrive. There are several forms, including 'Rosea' (pink) and 'Royal Star' (large and white). Grow in a moist, well-drained, neutral soil.

SPRING · SUMMER · AUTUMN · WINTER
10ft ↕ 12ft

MAHONIA JAPONICA **Z** 7–8
BERBERIDACEAE

A hardy evergreen shrub with leaves formed of dark, glossy, leathery, spine-edged, hollylike leaflets. The lemon-yellow flowers, with the fragrance of lily-of-the-valley, are borne in drooping clusters 6–9in (15–23cm) long from the tips of stems, from midwinter to early spring. These are followed by blue-purple berries. Grow in a fertile, moist, but well-drained soil.

SPRING · SUMMER · AUTUMN · WINTER
6ft ↕ 10ft

MAHONIA X MEDIA 'CHARITY' **Z** 8–9
BERBERIDACEAE

Previously known as *Mahonia* 'Charity', this is an ideal evergreen shrub for planting in a winter-flowering garden. It develops deep yellow, sweetly scented flowers in spires up to 12in (30cm) long from late autumn to late winter. The leaves are formed of spiny leaflets. Grow in a fertile, moist, but well-drained soil.

SPRING · SUMMER · AUTUMN · WINTER
15ft ↕ 12ft

MALUS FLORIBUNDA **Z** 4–8
FLOWERING CRAB APPLE
ROSACEAE

A distinctive, deciduous, round-headed and densely branched tree with mid-green leaves and masses of single, 1in (2.5cm) wide, pale pink flowers, carmine when in bud, during late spring. Later it bears masses of yellow fruits. Grow in a moderately fertile, moist, but well-drained soil.

SPRING · SUMMER · AUTUMN · WINTER
30ft ↕ 30ft

MALUS HUPEHENSIS **Z** 5–8
CRAB APPLE
ROSACEAE

This vigorous deciduous tree has attractive ovate, dark green leaves and in late spring and early summer it bears single, white flowers tinged rose-pink. These are eventually followed by red-tinted, yellow, long-lasting fruit. Ideal for a larger garden, this tree needs a moderately fertile, well-drained soil.

SPRING · SUMMER · AUTUMN · WINTER
40ft ↕ 40ft

OSMANTHUS X BURKWOODII **Z** 7–9
OLEACEAE

Earlier known as x *Osmarea burkwoodii*, this evergreen shrub has sweetly scented, white, tubular flowers borne in small clusters during mid- and late spring. These appear among mid- to dark green, glossy, and pointed leaves. This species can sometimes produce fruit. Grow in a fertile, well-drained soil.

SPRING · SUMMER · AUTUMN · WINTER
10ft ↕ 10ft

≣ leaf type　　　● light preference　　　♟ speed of growth　　　✿ ease of growth

PHILADELPHUS 'AVALANCHE' **Z** 5–8
MOCK ORANGE
HYDRANGEACEAE

A popular, small, deciduous shrub with a profusion of white, cup-shaped, single flowers in early and midsummer that have a richly sweet fragrance, with overtones of orange blossom. Often, the weight of the clusters bends down the branches. It likes a moderately fertile, moist, but well-drained soil.

5ft / 10ft

PHILADELPHUS 'BEAUCLERK' **Z** 5–8
MOCK ORANGE
HYDRANGEACEAE

A deciduous shrub with a slightly arching nature, this has oval, slightly tooth-edged leaves and large, cup-shaped white flowers flushed pink at their centers in early and midsummer. It is a good specimen plant. It requires a moderately fertile, moist, but well-drained soil.

8ft / 8ft

PHILADELPHUS 'VIRGINAL' **Z** 5–8
MOCK ORANGE
HYDRANGEACEAE

Earlier known as *Philadelphus* x *virginalis* 'Virginal', this superb deciduous shrub bears richly sweet flowers in early to midsummer. They are white, cup-shaped, 2in (5cm) wide, double or semidouble. When in flower it creates a dominant display. It requires a moderately fertile, moist, but well-drained soil.

10ft / 8ft

PONCIRUS TRIFOLIATA **Z** 5–9
BITTER ORANGE
RUTACEAE

A distinctive deciduous shrub or small tree which produces pure white flowers in late spring, each up to 2in (5cm) wide and with a sweet and orange-blossomlike fragrance. They are borne along bare, spiny stems before the leaves appear. Grow in fertile, well-drained soil.

15ft / 15ft

PRUNUS PADUS 'WATERERI' **Z** 4–8
BIRD CHERRY
ROSACEAE

A distinctive deciduous tree with small, white, almond-scented, 1/2 in (12mm) wide flowers borne in slender, drooping tassels up to 8in (20cm) long in late spring. These are followed by glossy black fruit. The tree's bark has a rather strong, acrid smell. Grow in soil which is moderately fertile and well drained.

50ft / 30ft

PRUNUS X YEDOENSIS **Z** 6–8
YOSHINO CHERRY
ROSACEAE

A graceful, deciduous, rounded and distinctive tree with blush-white, almond-scented flowers, up to 11/2 in (36mm) wide, in spring, borne in pendulous clusters. It is ideal for planting as a specimen tree in a large lawn. Grow in soil which is moderately fertile and well drained.

50ft / 30ft

↕ height and spread   ✳ feature of interest   ▮▮▮ season of interest   *TREES AND SHRUBS* **M – P**

TREES AND SHRUBS

RHODODENDRON LUTEUM ❷ 6–9
ERICACEAE

Earlier known as *Rhododendron flavum*, this is a superb deciduous shrub. It develops richly sweet, funnel-shaped, bright yellow flowers borne in large clusters in late spring and early summer. It is ideal for planting in a woodland garden or on a bank alongside a stream. Grow in a moist but well-drained, moderately fertile acid soil in a sheltered site.

12ft / 12ft

RIBES ODORATUM ❷ 5–8
BUFFALO CURRANT
GROSSULARIACEAE

A colorful deciduous shrub with bright, golden-yellow, semipendulous flowers in mid- and late spring that exude a delicious clove- and spicelike scent. These are followed by ovoid black fruit. The three-lobed pale green leaves often assume rich tints in autumn. This is a plant that likes fertile, well-drained soil.

6ft / 6ft

SKIMMIA JAPONICA 'FRAGRANS' ❷ 7–9
RUTACEAE

A widely grown evergreen shrub with pale green, leathery, oval to lance-shaped leaves. The starlike, white flowers, which are produced in mid- and late spring, are borne in 2–3in (5–7.5cm) long terminal clusters. They have a sweet fragrance, with a hint of lily-of-the-valley. Grow in a fertile, moist, well-drained soil.

3ft / 3ft

SPARTIUM JUNCEUM ❷ 8–10
SPANISH BROOM
PAPILIONACEAE

A distinctive deciduous shrub with rushlike green stems that create an evergreen appearance. Pea-shaped, bright golden-yellow flowers with a sweet, honeylike fragrance are borne along almost leafless stems from early to late summer, followed by dark brown seed pods. Grow in a well-drained soil.

10ft / 10ft

SYRINGA MICROPHYLLA ❷ 5–8
LILAC
OLEACEAE

A deciduous, small-leaved lilac with rosy-lilac flowers borne in 3–4in (7.5–10cm) long, erect clusters in early summer and again in early autumn. They have a penetrating lilac fragrance. 'Superba' has rose-pink flowers mainly in early summer, and intermittently until early autumn. Grow in a fertile, rich, and well-drained soil.

6ft / 6ft

SYRINGA VULGARIS ❷ 4–8
COMMON LILAC
OLEACEAE

A well-known deciduous, hardy shrub. The lilac flowers, produced in late spring and early summer, have a characteristic sweet scent and are borne in pyramidal clusters. There are many varieties, in colors including white, creamy-yellow, mauve, red, pink, and purple. Grow in a fertile, rich, well-drained soil.

22ft / 22ft

≣ leaf type   ● light preference   ⚡ speed of growth   ✿ ease of growth

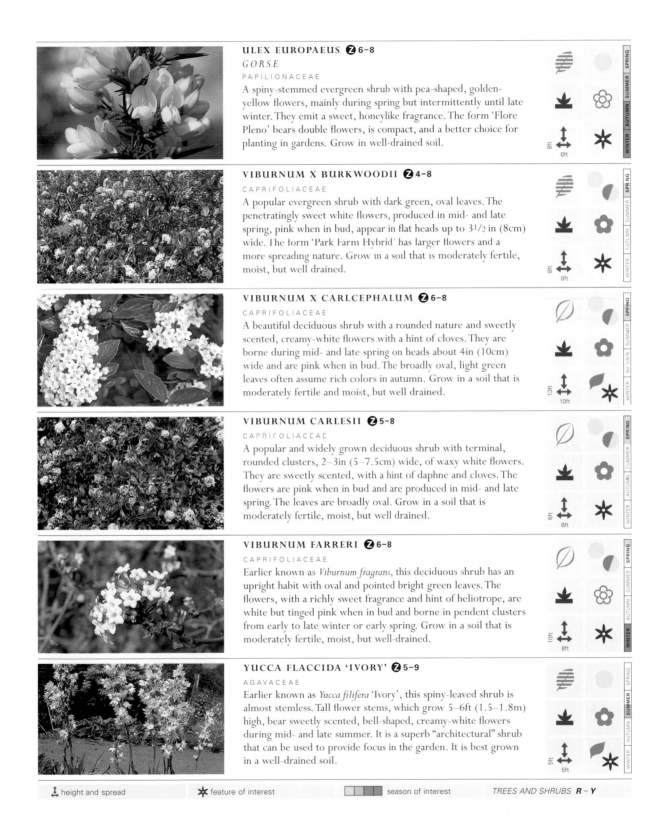

ULEX EUROPAEUS ✪ 6–8
GORSE
PAPILIONACEAE

A spiny-stemmed evergreen shrub with pea-shaped, golden-yellow flowers, mainly during spring but intermittently until late winter. They emit a sweet, honeylike fragrance. The form 'Flore Pleno' bears double flowers, is compact, and a better choice for planting in gardens. Grow in well-drained soil.

VIBURNUM X BURKWOODII ✪ 4–8
CAPRIFOLIACEAE

A popular evergreen shrub with dark green, oval leaves. The penetratingly sweet white flowers, produced in mid- and late spring, pink when in bud, appear in flat heads up to 3¹/₂ in (8cm) wide. The form 'Park Farm Hybrid' has larger flowers and a more spreading nature. Grow in a soil that is moderately fertile, moist, but well drained.

VIBURNUM X CARLCEPHALUM ✪ 6–8
CAPRIFOLIACEAE

A beautiful deciduous shrub with a rounded nature and sweetly scented, creamy-white flowers with a hint of cloves. They are borne during mid- and late spring on heads about 4in (10cm) wide and are pink when in bud. The broadly oval, light green leaves often assume rich colors in autumn. Grow in a soil that is moderately fertile and moist, but well drained.

VIBURNUM CARLESII ✪ 5–8
CAPRIFOLIACEAE

A popular and widely grown deciduous shrub with terminal, rounded clusters, 2–3in (5–7.5cm) wide, of waxy white flowers. They are sweetly scented, with a hint of daphne and cloves. The flowers are pink when in bud and are produced in mid- and late spring. The leaves are broadly oval. Grow in a soil that is moderately fertile, moist, but well drained.

VIBURNUM FARRERI ✪ 6–8
CAPRIFOLIACEAE

Earlier known as *Viburnum fragrans*, this deciduous shrub has an upright habit with oval and pointed bright green leaves. The flowers, with a richly sweet fragrance and hint of heliotrope, are white but tinged pink when in bud and borne in pendent clusters from early to late winter or early spring. Grow in a soil that is moderately fertile, moist, but well-drained.

YUCCA FLACCIDA 'IVORY' ✪ 5–9
AGAVACEAE

Earlier known as *Yucca filifera* 'Ivory', this spiny-leaved shrub is almost stemless. Tall flower stems, which grow 5–6ft (1.5–1.8m) high, bear sweetly scented, bell-shaped, creamy-white flowers during mid- and late summer. It is a superb "architectural" shrub that can be used to provide focus in the garden. It is best grown in a well-drained soil.

⬍ height and spread   ✱ feature of interest   ▮▮▮ season of interest   *TREES AND SHRUBS* **R – Y**

ANNUALS AND BIENNIALS FOR HERB GARDENS

ANETHUM GRAVEOLENS **Z** 2–9
DILL
APIACEAE

Earlier known as *Peucedanum graveolens*, this popular annual culinary herb has threadlike, bluish-green leaves that emit an aniselike and spicy fragrance. The seeds have a similar scent, but with a hint of caraway. Tiny yellow flowers appear throughout summer. Grow in a fertile, well-drained soil, in a sheltered site.

24in / 12in

ANGELICA ARCHANGELICA **Z** 4–9
ANGELICA
APIACEAE

A distinctive culinary herb, this biennial has light green, fine tooth-edged, and deeply dissected leaves which have a musklike scent, with a hint of juniper. The seeds also have a musklike bouquet. Produces greenish-yellow flowers in mid- and late summer. Grow in a moist, loamy, and fertile soil.

6ft / 4ft

ANTHRISCUS CEREFOLIUM **Z** 3–7
CHERVIL
APIACEAE

This biennial culinary herb has bright green, finely divided, fernlike leaves that have a distinctive aniselike scent. The hollow stems are also aromatic. It develops white flowers throughout summer in the plant's second year. Good for a herbaceous border, it prefers well-drained soil in either sun or partial shade.

20in / 10in

BORAGO OFFICINALIS **Z** 3–9
BORAGE
BORAGINACEAE

A well-known culinary herb, this annual has oval, corrugated leaves that, when bruised, have the redolence of cucumber. The blue, starlike flowers, which appear throughout summer, also reveal this scent. There are pink- and white-flowered forms. Needs a moist soil and prefers full sun.

24in / 18in

CALENDULA OFFICINALIS **Z** 3–11
ENGLISH MARIGOLD
ASTERACEAE

A popular hardy annual, earlier used medicinally and culinarily, with leaves and stems that reveal a pungent aroma when bruised. The large, daisylike, orange or yellow flowers appear from late spring to autumn. An excellent annual for a border. Choose a soil that is well drained and moderately fertile.

12–30in / 12–18in

CARUM CARVI **Z** 3–9
CARAWAY
APIACEAE

A popular biennial culinary herb with mid-green, fernlike leaves that have a sweet scent. The seeds have the fragrance of a fusion of caraway and licorice. Small green flowers in early and midsummer. Often grown as part of a herb garden, this species likes a fertile, well-drained soil.

24in / 12in

| ≣ leaf type | ● light preference | ♨ speed of growth | ✿ ease of growth |

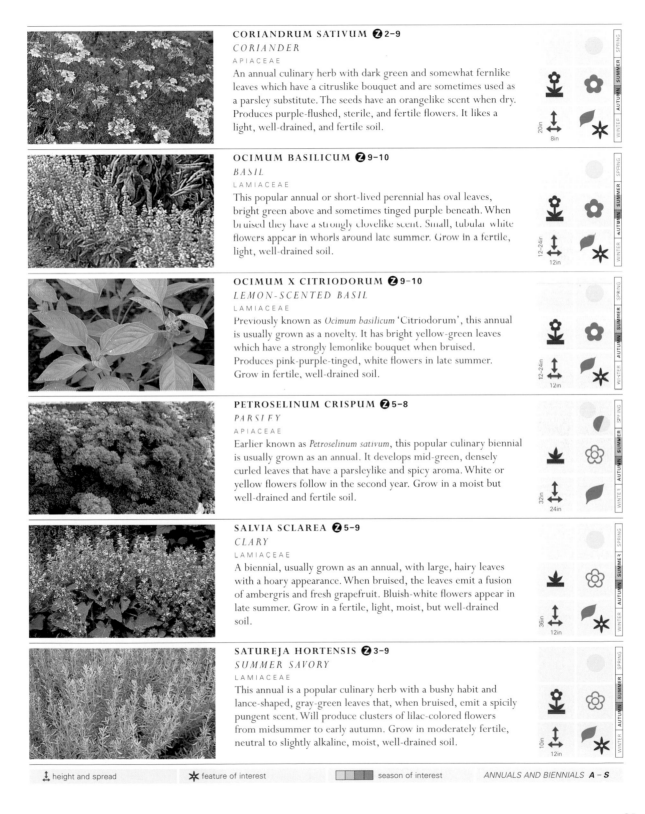

CORIANDRUM SATIVUM **Z** 2–9
CORIANDER
APIACEAE

An annual culinary herb with dark green and somewhat fernlike leaves which have a citruslike bouquet and are sometimes used as a parsley substitute. The seeds have an orangelike scent when dry. Produces purple-flushed, sterile, and fertile flowers. It likes a light, well-drained, and fertile soil.

20in / 8in

OCIMUM BASILICUM **Z** 9–10
BASIL
LAMIACEAE

This popular annual or short-lived perennial has oval leaves, bright green above and sometimes tinged purple beneath. When bruised they have a strongly clovelike scent. Small, tubular white flowers appear in whorls around late summer. Grow in a fertile, light, well-drained soil.

12–24in / 12in

OCIMUM X CITRIODORUM **Z** 9–10
LEMON-SCENTED BASIL
LAMIACEAE

Previously known as *Ocimum basilicum* 'Citriodorum', this annual is usually grown as a novelty. It has bright yellow-green leaves which have a strongly lemonlike bouquet when bruised. Produces pink-purple-tinged, white flowers in late summer. Grow in fertile, well-drained soil.

12–24in / 12in

PETROSELINUM CRISPUM **Z** 5–8
PARSLEY
APIACEAE

Earlier known as *Petroselinum sativum*, this popular culinary biennial is usually grown as an annual. It develops mid-green, densely curled leaves that have a parsleylike and spicy aroma. White or yellow flowers follow in the second year. Grow in a moist but well-drained and fertile soil.

32in / 24in

SALVIA SCLAREA **Z** 5–9
CLARY
LAMIACEAE

A biennial, usually grown as an annual, with large, hairy leaves with a hoary appearance. When bruised, the leaves emit a fusion of ambergris and fresh grapefruit. Bluish-white flowers appear in late summer. Grow in a fertile, light, moist, but well-drained soil.

36in / 12in

SATUREJA HORTENSIS **Z** 3–9
SUMMER SAVORY
LAMIACEAE

This annual is a popular culinary herb with a bushy habit and lance-shaped, gray-green leaves that, when bruised, emit a spicily pungent scent. Will produce clusters of lilac-colored flowers from midsummer to early autumn. Grow in moderately fertile, neutral to slightly alkaline, moist, well-drained soil.

10in / 12in

↕ height and spread   ✳ feature of interest   ▭▭▭ season of interest   *ANNUALS AND BIENNIALS* **A – S**

SCENTED-LEAVED PELARGONIUMS

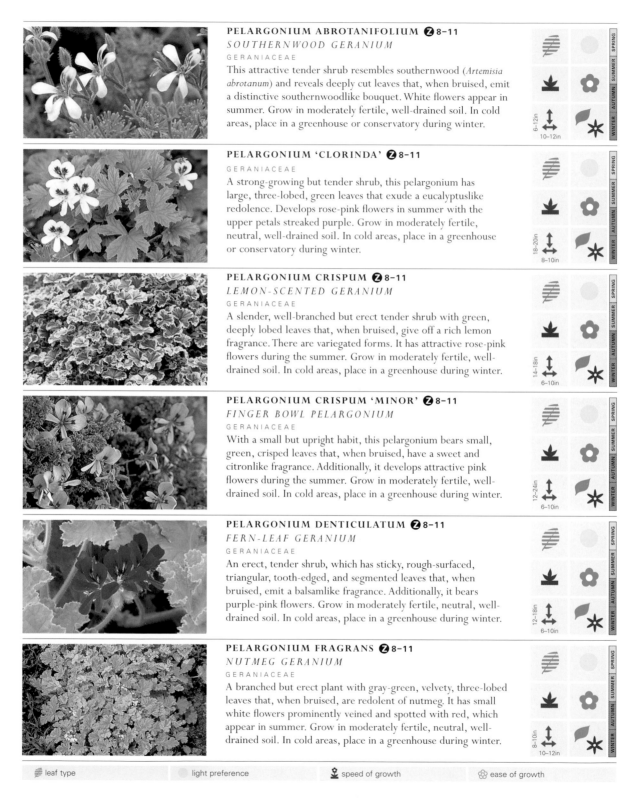

PELARGONIUM ABROTANIFOLIUM ❷ 8–11
SOUTHERNWOOD GERANIUM
GERANIACEAE
This attractive tender shrub resembles southernwood (*Artemisia abrotanum*) and reveals deeply cut leaves that, when bruised, emit a distinctive southernwoodlike bouquet. White flowers appear in summer. Grow in moderately fertile, well-drained soil. In cold areas, place in a greenhouse or conservatory during winter.

6–12in
10–12in
SPRING SUMMER AUTUMN WINTER

PELARGONIUM 'CLORINDA' ❷ 8–11
GERANIACEAE
A strong-growing but tender shrub, this pelargonium has large, three-lobed, green leaves that exude a eucalyptuslike redolence. Develops rose-pink flowers in summer with the upper petals streaked purple. Grow in moderately fertile, neutral, well-drained soil. In cold areas, place in a greenhouse or conservatory during winter.

18–20in
8–10in
SPRING SUMMER AUTUMN WINTER

PELARGONIUM CRISPUM ❷ 8–11
LEMON-SCENTED GERANIUM
GERANIACEAE
A slender, well-branched but erect tender shrub with green, deeply lobed leaves that, when bruised, give off a rich lemon fragrance. There are variegated forms. It has attractive rose-pink flowers during the summer. Grow in moderately fertile, well-drained soil. In cold areas, place in a greenhouse during winter.

14–18in
6–10in
SPRING SUMMER AUTUMN WINTER

PELARGONIUM CRISPUM 'MINOR' ❷ 8–11
FINGER BOWL PELARGONIUM
GERANIACEAE
With a small but upright habit, this pelargonium bears small, green, crisped leaves that, when bruised, have a sweet and citronlike fragrance. Additionally, it develops attractive pink flowers during the summer. Grow in moderately fertile, well-drained soil. In cold areas, place in a greenhouse during winter.

12–24in
6–10in
SPRING SUMMER AUTUMN WINTER

PELARGONIUM DENTICULATUM ❷ 8–11
FERN-LEAF GERANIUM
GERANIACEAE
An erect, tender shrub, which has sticky, rough-surfaced, triangular, tooth-edged, and segmented leaves that, when bruised, emit a balsamlike fragrance. Additionally, it bears purple-pink flowers. Grow in moderately fertile, neutral, well-drained soil. In cold areas, place in a greenhouse during winter.

12–18in
6–10in
SPRING SUMMER AUTUMN WINTER

PELARGONIUM FRAGRANS ❷ 8–11
NUTMEG GERANIUM
GERANIACEAE
A branched but erect plant with gray-green, velvety, three-lobed leaves that, when bruised, are redolent of nutmeg. It has small white flowers prominently veined and spotted with red, which appear in summer. Grow in moderately fertile, neutral, well-drained soil. In cold areas, place in a greenhouse during winter.

8–10in
10–12in
SPRING SUMMER AUTUMN WINTER

leaf type   light preference   speed of growth   ease of growth

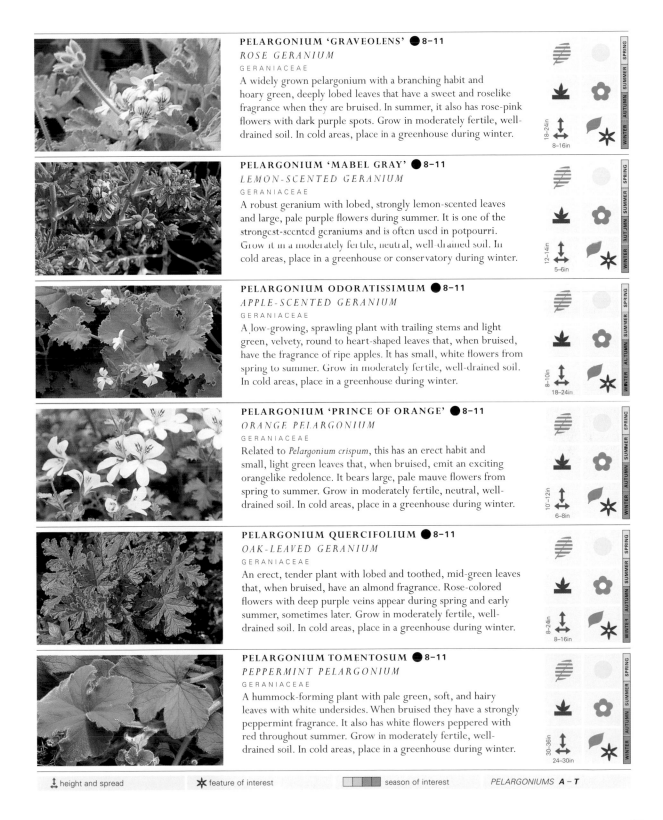

PELARGONIUM 'GRAVEOLENS' ●8–11
ROSE GERANIUM
GERANIACEAE

A widely grown pelargonium with a branching habit and hoary green, deeply lobed leaves that have a sweet and roselike fragrance when they are bruised. In summer, it also has rose-pink flowers with dark purple spots. Grow in moderately fertile, well-drained soil. In cold areas, place in a greenhouse during winter.

18–24in
8–16in
SPRING SUMMER AUTUMN WINTER

PELARGONIUM 'MABEL GRAY' ●8–11
LEMON-SCENTED GERANIUM
GERANIACEAE

A robust geranium with lobed, strongly lemon-scented leaves and large, pale purple flowers during summer. It is one of the strongest-scented geraniums and is often used in potpourri. Grow it in a moderately fertile, neutral, well-drained soil. In cold areas, place in a greenhouse or conservatory during winter.

12–14in
5–6in
SPRING SUMMER AUTUMN WINTER

PELARGONIUM ODORATISSIMUM ●8–11
APPLE-SCENTED GERANIUM
GERANIACEAE

A low-growing, sprawling plant with trailing stems and light green, velvety, round to heart-shaped leaves that, when bruised, have the fragrance of ripe apples. It has small, white flowers from spring to summer. Grow in moderately fertile, well-drained soil. In cold areas, place in a greenhouse during winter.

8–10in
18–24in
SPRING SUMMER AUTUMN WINTER

PELARGONIUM 'PRINCE OF ORANGE' ●8–11
ORANGE PELARGONIUM
GERANIACEAE

Related to *Pelargonium crispum*, this has an erect habit and small, light green leaves that, when bruised, emit an exciting orangelike redolence. It bears large, pale mauve flowers from spring to summer. Grow in moderately fertile, neutral, well-drained soil. In cold areas, place in a greenhouse during winter.

10–12in
6–8in
SPRING SUMMER AUTUMN WINTER

PELARGONIUM QUERCIFOLIUM ●8–11
OAK-LEAVED GERANIUM
GERANIACEAE

An erect, tender plant with lobed and toothed, mid-green leaves that, when bruised, have an almond fragrance. Rose-colored flowers with deep purple veins appear during spring and early summer, sometimes later. Grow in moderately fertile, well-drained soil. In cold areas, place in a greenhouse during winter.

8–24in
8–16in
SPRING SUMMER AUTUMN WINTER

PELARGONIUM TOMENTOSUM ●8–11
PEPPERMINT PELARGONIUM
GERANIACEAE

A hummock-forming plant with pale green, soft, and hairy leaves with white undersides. When bruised they have a strongly peppermint fragrance. It also has white flowers peppered with red throughout summer. Grow in moderately fertile, well-drained soil. In cold areas, place in a greenhouse during winter.

30–36in
24–30in
SPRING SUMMER AUTUMN WINTER

⬍ height and spread   ✳ feature of interest   ▭▭▭ season of interest   *PELARGONIUMS A – T*

HERBACEOUS PERENNIALS

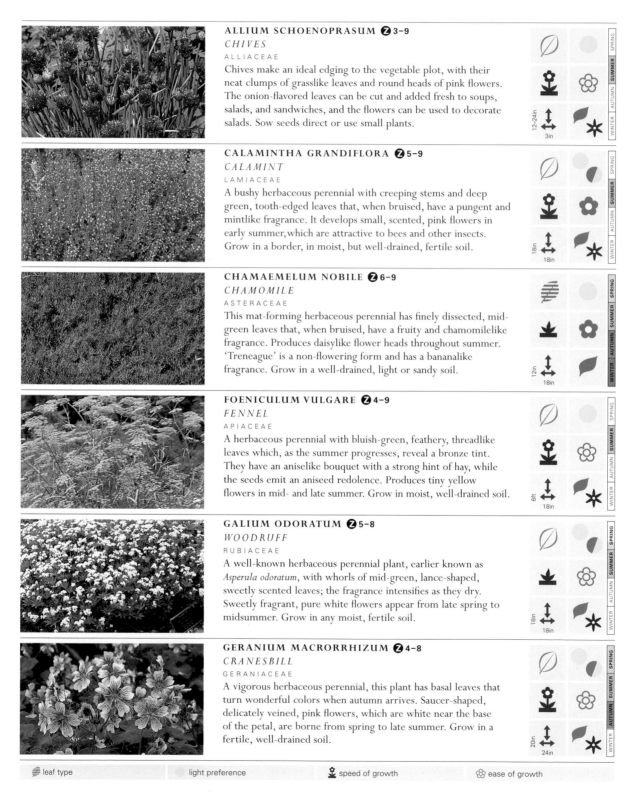

ALLIUM SCHOENOPRASUM ❷ 3–9

CHIVES

ALLIACEAE

Chives make an ideal edging to the vegetable plot, with their neat clumps of grasslike leaves and round heads of pink flowers. The onion-flavored leaves can be cut and added fresh to soups, salads, and sandwiches, and the flowers can be used to decorate salads. Sow seeds direct or use small plants.

12–24in • 3in

CALAMINTHA GRANDIFLORA ❷ 5–9

CALAMINT

LAMIACEAE

A bushy herbaceous perennial with creeping stems and deep green, tooth-edged leaves that, when bruised, have a pungent and mintlike fragrance. It develops small, scented, pink flowers in early summer, which are attractive to bees and other insects. Grow in a border, in moist, but well-drained, fertile soil.

18in • 18in

CHAMAEMELUM NOBILE ❷ 6–9

CHAMOMILE

ASTERACEAE

This mat-forming herbaceous perennial has finely dissected, mid-green leaves that, when bruised, have a fruity and chamomilelike fragrance. Produces daisylike flower heads throughout summer. 'Treneague' is a non-flowering form and has a bananalike fragrance. Grow in a well-drained, light or sandy soil.

12in • 18in

FOENICULUM VULGARE ❷ 4–9

FENNEL

APIACEAE

A herbaceous perennial with bluish-green, feathery, threadlike leaves which, as the summer progresses, reveal a bronze tint. They have an aniselike bouquet with a strong hint of hay, while the seeds emit an aniseed redolence. Produces tiny yellow flowers in mid- and late summer. Grow in moist, well-drained soil.

6ft • 18in

GALIUM ODORATUM ❷ 5–8

WOODRUFF

RUBIACEAE

A well-known herbaceous perennial plant, earlier known as *Asperula odoratum*, with whorls of mid-green, lance-shaped, sweetly scented leaves; the fragrance intensifies as they dry. Sweetly fragrant, pure white flowers appear from late spring to midsummer. Grow in any moist, fertile soil.

18in • 18in

GERANIUM MACRORRHIZUM ❷ 4–8

CRANESBILL

GERANIACEAE

A vigorous herbaceous perennial, this plant has basal leaves that turn wonderful colors when autumn arrives. Saucer-shaped, delicately veined, pink flowers, which are white near the base of the petal, are borne from spring to late summer. Grow in a fertile, well-drained soil.

20in • 24in

SPRING | SUMMER | AUTUMN | WINTER

≣ leaf type   ● light preference   ⚘ speed of growth   ❀ ease of growth

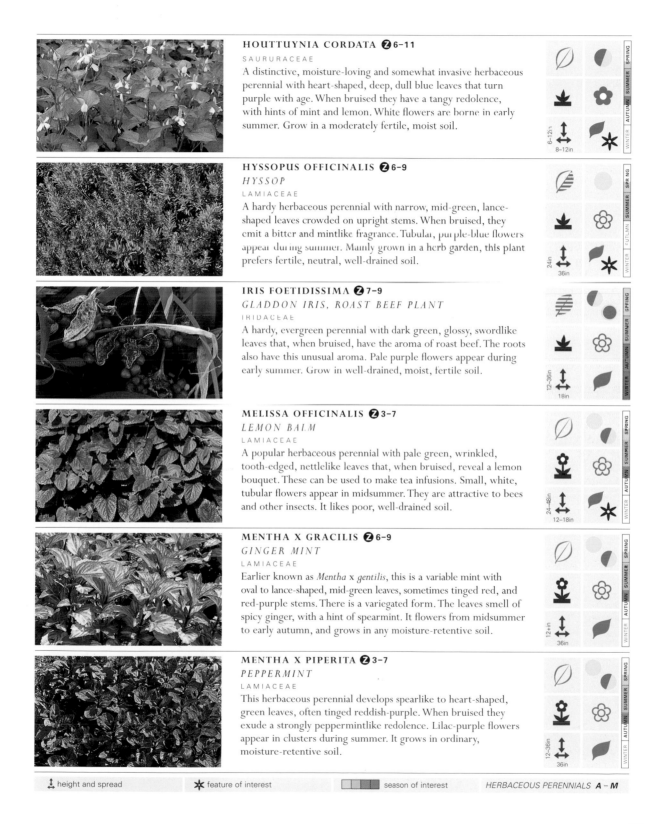

HOUTTUYNIA CORDATA ⓩ 6–11
SAURURACEAE

A distinctive, moisture-loving and somewhat invasive herbaceous perennial with heart-shaped, deep, dull blue leaves that turn purple with age. When bruised they have a tangy redolence, with hints of mint and lemon. White flowers are borne in early summer. Grow in a moderately fertile, moist soil.

6–12in / 8–12in

HYSSOPUS OFFICINALIS ⓩ 6–9
HYSSOP
LAMIACEAE

A hardy herbaceous perennial with narrow, mid-green, lance-shaped leaves crowded on upright stems. When bruised, they emit a bitter and mintlike fragrance. Tubular, purple-blue flowers appear during summer. Mainly grown in a herb garden, this plant prefers fertile, neutral, well-drained soil.

24in / 36in

IRIS FOETIDISSIMA ⓩ 7–9
GLADDON IRIS, ROAST BEEF PLANT
IRIDACEAE

A hardy, evergreen perennial with dark green, glossy, swordlike leaves that, when bruised, have the aroma of roast beef. The roots also have this unusual aroma. Pale purple flowers appear during early summer. Grow in well-drained, moist, fertile soil.

12–36in / 18in

MELISSA OFFICINALIS ⓩ 3–7
LEMON BALM
LAMIACEAE

A popular herbaceous perennial with pale green, wrinkled, tooth-edged, nettlelike leaves that, when bruised, reveal a lemon bouquet. These can be used to make tea infusions. Small, white, tubular flowers appear in midsummer. They are attractive to bees and other insects. It likes poor, well-drained soil.

24–48in / 12–18in

MENTHA X GRACILIS ⓩ 6–9
GINGER MINT
LAMIACEAE

Earlier known as *Mentha* x *gentilis*, this is a variable mint with oval to lance-shaped, mid-green leaves, sometimes tinged red, and red-purple stems. There is a variegated form. The leaves smell of spicy ginger, with a hint of spearmint. It flowers from midsummer to early autumn, and grows in any moisture-retentive soil.

12+in / 36in

MENTHA X PIPERITA ⓩ 3–7
PEPPERMINT
LAMIACEAE

This herbaceous perennial develops spearlike to heart-shaped, green leaves, often tinged reddish-purple. When bruised they exude a strongly peppermintlike redolence. Lilac-purple flowers appear in clusters during summer. It grows in ordinary, moisture-retentive soil.

12–36in / 36in

↕ height and spread   ✳ feature of interest   ▭ season of interest   *HERBACEOUS PERENNIALS* **A – M**

HERBACEOUS PERENNIALS

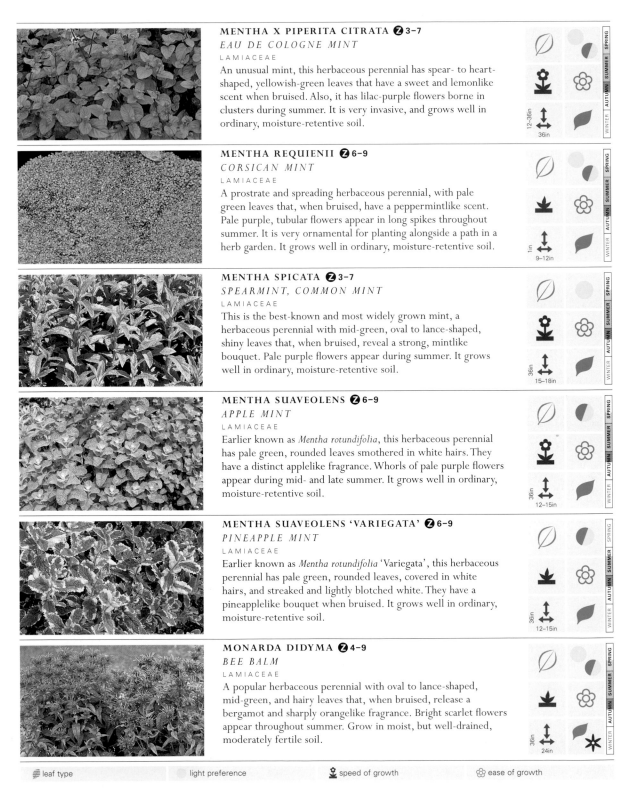

MENTHA X PIPERITA CITRATA ❷ 3–7
EAU DE COLOGNE MINT
LAMIACEAE

An unusual mint, this herbaceous perennial has spear- to heart-shaped, yellowish-green leaves that have a sweet and lemonlike scent when bruised. Also, it has lilac-purple flowers borne in clusters during summer. It is very invasive, and grows well in ordinary, moisture-retentive soil.

MENTHA REQUIENII ❷ 6–9
CORSICAN MINT
LAMIACEAE

A prostrate and spreading herbaceous perennial, with pale green leaves that, when bruised, have a peppermintlike scent. Pale purple, tubular flowers appear in long spikes throughout summer. It is very ornamental for planting alongside a path in a herb garden. It grows well in ordinary, moisture-retentive soil.

MENTHA SPICATA ❷ 3–7
SPEARMINT, COMMON MINT
LAMIACEAE

This is the best-known and most widely grown mint, a herbaceous perennial with mid-green, oval to lance-shaped, shiny leaves that, when bruised, reveal a strong, mintlike bouquet. Pale purple flowers appear during summer. It grows well in ordinary, moisture-retentive soil.

MENTHA SUAVEOLENS ❷ 6–9
APPLE MINT
LAMIACEAE

Earlier known as *Mentha rotundifolia*, this herbaceous perennial has pale green, rounded leaves smothered in white hairs. They have a distinct applelike fragrance. Whorls of pale purple flowers appear during mid- and late summer. It grows well in ordinary, moisture-retentive soil.

MENTHA SUAVEOLENS 'VARIEGATA' ❷ 6–9
PINEAPPLE MINT
LAMIACEAE

Earlier known as *Mentha rotundifolia* 'Variegata', this herbaceous perennial has pale green, rounded leaves, covered in white hairs, and streaked and lightly blotched white. They have a pineapplelike bouquet when bruised. It grows well in ordinary, moisture-retentive soil.

MONARDA DIDYMA ❷ 4–9
BEE BALM
LAMIACEAE

A popular herbaceous perennial with oval to lance-shaped, mid-green, and hairy leaves that, when bruised, release a bergamot and sharply orangelike fragrance. Bright scarlet flowers appear throughout summer. Grow in moist, but well-drained, moderately fertile soil.

≣ leaf type   ◐ light preference   ♟ speed of growth   ✿ ease of growth

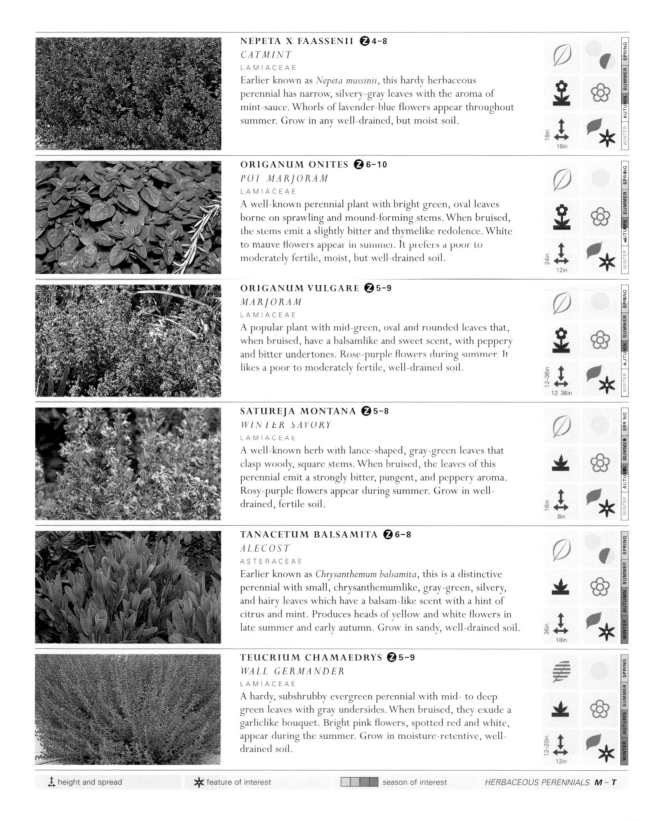

NEPETA X FAASSENII ✐ 4–8
CATMINT
LAMIACEAE
Earlier known as *Nepeta mussinii*, this hardy herbaceous perennial has narrow, silvery-gray leaves with the aroma of mint-sauce. Whorls of lavender-blue flowers appear throughout summer. Grow in any well-drained, but moist soil.

ORIGANUM ONITES ✐ 6–10
POT MARJORAM
LAMIACEAE
A well-known perennial plant with bright green, oval leaves borne on sprawling and mound-forming stems. When bruised, the stems emit a slightly bitter and thymelike redolence. White to mauve flowers appear in summer. It prefers a poor to moderately fertile, moist, but well-drained soil.

ORIGANUM VULGARE ✐ 5–9
MARJORAM
LAMIACEAE
A popular plant with mid-green, oval and rounded leaves that, when bruised, have a balsamlike and sweet scent, with peppery and bitter undertones. Rose-purple flowers during summer. It likes a poor to moderately fertile, well-drained soil.

SATUREJA MONTANA ✐ 5–8
WINTER SAVORY
LAMIACEAE
A well-known herb with lance-shaped, gray-green leaves that clasp woody, square stems. When bruised, the leaves of this perennial emit a strongly bitter, pungent, and peppery aroma. Rosy-purple flowers appear during summer. Grow in well-drained, fertile soil.

TANACETUM BALSAMITA ✐ 6–8
ALECOST
ASTERACEAE
Earlier known as *Chrysanthemum balsamita*, this is a distinctive perennial with small, chrysanthemumlike, gray-green, silvery, and hairy leaves which have a balsam-like scent with a hint of citrus and mint. Produces heads of yellow and white flowers in late summer and early autumn. Grow in sandy, well-drained soil.

TEUCRIUM CHAMAEDRYS ✐ 5–9
WALL GERMANDER
LAMIACEAE
A hardy, subshrubby evergreen perennial with mid- to deep green leaves with gray undersides. When bruised, they exude a garliclike bouquet. Bright pink flowers, spotted red and white, appear during the summer. Grow in moisture-retentive, well-drained soil.

↕ height and spread   ✷ feature of interest   ▭▭▭▭ season of interest   *HERBACEOUS PERENNIALS* **M – T**

TREES AND SHRUBS

ALOYSIA TRIPHYLLA **Z** 8–11
LEMON VERBENA
VERBENACEAE

Earlier known as *Lippia citriodora*, this deciduous shrub has pale to mid-green, lance-shaped leaves that, when bruised, have a strongly lemon fragrance. Also, it develops pale mauve flowers in late summer. The leaves have been widely used in perfumery. It grows in light, well-drained soil.

ARTEMISIA ABSINTHIUM **Z** 4–8
COMMON WORMWOOD
ASTERACEAE

A subshrubby and deciduous shrub with silvery-gray, finely divided leaves that have a sharp fragrance, with a hint of absinthe and sweetness. It has small, round, yellow flowers during mid- and late summer, and is ideal for planting in a shrub or mixed border. Choose a soil that is well drained and moderately fertile.

CARYOPTERIS X CLANDONENSIS **Z** 6–9
BLUE SPIRAEA
VERBENACEAE

A half-hardy deciduous shrub with narrow, gray-green leaves that, when bruised, have a strong and pungent aroma. Bright blue, tubular flowers appear during late summer and into early autumn. Good for a shrub border. Grow in light, moderately fertile, well-drained soil.

CHOISYA TERNATA **Z** 8–10
MEXICAN ORANGE BLOSSOM
RUTACEAE

An evergreen shrub with glossy leaves that, when bruised, have an orangelike fragrance. The white, orange-blossomlike flowers, which arrive in late spring and intermittently to early winter, have a delicate orange scent. It likes a moderately fertile, well-drained soil.

CISTUS LADANIFER **Z** 8–10
COMMON GUM CISTUS
CISTACEAE

A hardy evergreen shrub with leathery, dull green leaves that have a richly gumlike scent with a hint of balsam, especially during warm evenings. It has white flowers with chocolate-maroon blotches in early summer. Grow in a poor, well-drained soil in a sheltered site.

ESCALLONIA MACRANTHA **Z** 8–9
ESCALLONIACEAE

Also known as *Escallonia rubra macrantha*, it forms a rounded evergreen shrub with oval to pear-shaped, glossy, deep green, tooth-edged leaves that have a pungent smell. The rose-crimson flowers, again with a pungent scent, are borne in terminal clusters. Plant it in a well-drained soil. Use in a border or as a hedge. It is also good in coastal conditions.

leaf type	light preference	speed of growth	ease of growth

GAULTHERIA PROCUMBENS ⓩ 3–8
WINTERGREEN
ERICACEAE

A creeping, ground-covering evergreen shrub with shiny, dark green leaves that cluster at the ends of stems. They have the fragrance of wintergreen. White or pink flowers appear in mid- and late summer. It is ideal for planting at the front of a shrub border. Grow in slightly acid, moist soil.

LAURUS NOBILIS ⓩ 8–10
SWEET BAY
LAURACEAE

A hardy evergreen shrub or small tree with glossy, lance-shaped, thick, mid- to dark green leaves that, when bruised, reveal a characteristic, slightly sweet aroma. Yellow-green flowers appear in late spring. A good specimen plant. Grow in moderately fertile, moist, but well-drained soil.

LAVANDULA ANGUSTIFOLIA ⓩ 5–8
LAVENDER
LAMIACEAE

A hardy evergreen shrub, earlier known as *Lavandula spica*, with narrow, silvery-gray, aromatic leaves with a characteristic fragrance. Fragrant, pale blue flowers appear in spikes from midsummer to autumn. Good for the base of a sunny wall or for a container. It thrives in moderately fertile, well-drained soil.

LAVANDULA STOECHAS ⓩ 8–9
FRENCH LAVENDER, SPANISH LAVENDER
LAMIACEAE

A slightly tender evergreen shrub with grayish-green, narrow leaves that exude a lavenderlike bouquet, with a hint of pine. Tufts of dark purple, fragrant flowers appear during early and midsummer. This plant enjoys a moderately fertile, well-drained soil.

OLEARIA MACRODONTA ⓩ 9–10
DAISY BUSH
ASTERACEAE

A distinctive evergreen shrub with gray-green, hollylike leaves with white felt on their undersides. They have a strong musklike scent when bruised. Honey-scented white flowers appear during early and midsummer. Good as a hedge or a windbreak. Grow in moderately fertile, well-drained soil.

PEROVSKIA ATRIPLICIFOLIA ⓩ 6–9
LAMIACEAE

A shrubby perennial with a herbaceous nature which forms an upright shrub with aromatic gray-green leaves and violet-blue flowers during late summer and early autumn. Because it is usually severely pruned in spring, it is often grown as part of a herbaceous border. It grows well in any light and well-drained soil.

⭤ height and spread   ✳ feature of interest   ▭▭▭▭ season of interest   *TREES AND SHRUBS* **A – P**

TREES AND SHRUBS

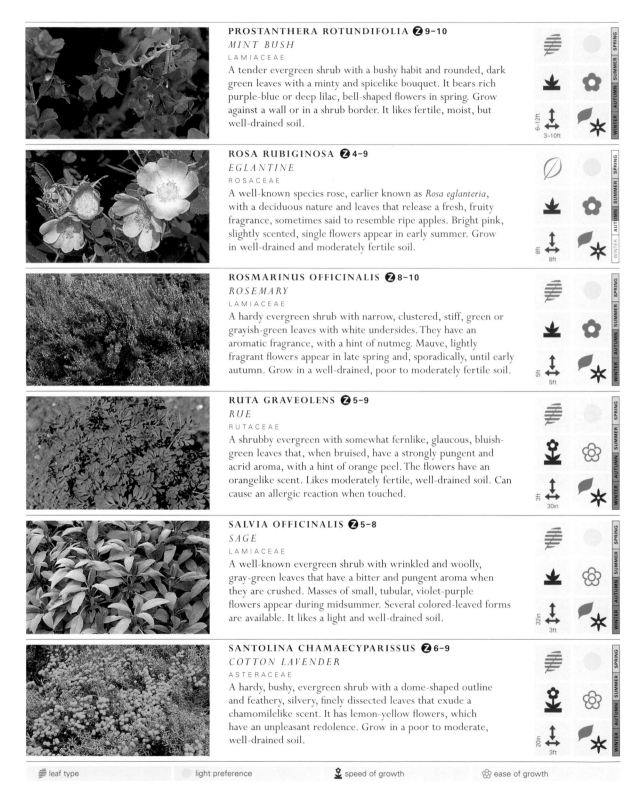

PROSTANTHERA ROTUNDIFOLIA Ⓩ 9–10
MINT BUSH
LAMIACEAE

A tender evergreen shrub with a bushy habit and rounded, dark green leaves with a minty and spicelike bouquet. It bears rich purple-blue or deep lilac, bell-shaped flowers in spring. Grow against a wall or in a shrub border. It likes fertile, moist, but well-drained soil.

6–12ft
3–10ft

ROSA RUBIGINOSA Ⓩ 4–9
EGLANTINE
ROSACEAE

A well-known species rose, earlier known as *Rosa eglanteria*, with a deciduous nature and leaves that release a fresh, fruity fragrance, sometimes said to resemble ripe apples. Bright pink, slightly scented, single flowers appear in early summer. Grow in well-drained and moderately fertile soil.

8ft
8ft

ROSMARINUS OFFICINALIS Ⓩ 8–10
ROSEMARY
LAMIACEAE

A hardy evergreen shrub with narrow, clustered, stiff, green or grayish-green leaves with white undersides. They have an aromatic fragrance, with a hint of nutmeg. Mauve, lightly fragrant flowers appear in late spring and, sporadically, until early autumn. Grow in a well-drained, poor to moderately fertile soil.

5ft
5ft

RUTA GRAVEOLENS Ⓩ 5–9
RUE
RUTACEAE

A shrubby evergreen with somewhat fernlike, glaucous, bluish-green leaves that, when bruised, have a strongly pungent and acrid aroma, with a hint of orange peel. The flowers have an orangelike scent. Likes moderately fertile, well-drained soil. Can cause an allergic reaction when touched.

3ft
30in

SALVIA OFFICINALIS Ⓩ 5–8
SAGE
LAMIACEAE

A well-known evergreen shrub with wrinkled and woolly, gray-green leaves that have a bitter and pungent aroma when they are crushed. Masses of small, tubular, violet-purple flowers appear during midsummer. Several colored-leaved forms are available. It likes a light and well-drained soil.

32in
3ft

SANTOLINA CHAMAECYPARISSUS Ⓩ 6–9
COTTON LAVENDER
ASTERACEAE

A hardy, bushy, evergreen shrub with a dome-shaped outline and feathery, silvery, finely dissected leaves that exude a chamomilelike scent. It has lemon-yellow flowers, which have an unpleasant redolence. Grow in a poor to moderate, well-drained soil.

20in
3ft

SPRING SUMMER AUTUMN WINTER

leaf type | light preference | speed of growth | ease of growth

SERIPHIDIUM TRIDENTATUM ❷ 8–9
BASIL SAGEBRUSH, SAGE BRUSH
ASTERACEAE

Earlier known as *Artemisia tridentata*, this hardy evergreen shrub has tapering, wedge-shaped leaves covered with a silvery-gray felt. They emit an intensely sweet fragrance, especially after a shower of rain. A good plant for a shrub border. Grow in poor to moderate, dry, and well-drained soil.

8ft / 8ft

THYMUS CAMPHORATUS ❷ 5–9
CAMPHOR THYME
LAMIACEAE

A hardy and somewhat straggly evergreen shrub with small, narrowly oval, dark green leaves with woolly upper sides. They have a camphorlike redolence. Purple-green flowers appear in midsummer and are very attractive to bees. This plant likes well-drained soil.

6–12in / 8–15in

THYMUS X CITRIODORUS ❷ 6–9
LEMON THYME
LAMIACEAE

A hardy, dwarf, evergreen shrub with mid-green, lance-shaped or nearly oval leaves that reveal a refreshing lemonlike fragrance when bruised. Small, pale lilac flowers appear in terminal clusters throughout summer. Attractive to bees. It likes dry, well-drained soil.

12in / 10in

THYMUS HERBA-BARONA ❷ 6–9
CARAWAY THYME
LAMIACEAE

A prostrate and mat-forming hardy evergreen shrub with dark green, lance-shaped leaves with a distinctive caraway fragrance when they are bruised. Tubular, pale lilac flowers appear in clusters during early summer. Attractive to bees. It likes dry, well-drained soil.

4in / 8in

THYMUS SERPYLLUM ❷ 4–9
ENGLISH THYME, WILD THYME
LAMIACEAE

A prostrate and hardy evergreen shrub with narrow, gray-green leaves that have the well-known fragrance of thyme. There are several varieties in a wide color range, from red through pink to white, throughout summer. Attractive to bees. It likes dry, well-drained soil.

10in / 18in

THYMUS VULGARIS ❷ 4–9
COMMON THYME
LAMIACEAE

A hardy, sprawling evergreen shrub bearing dark green, long, and narrow leaves that have a characteristic slightly sweet, pungent, and spicy aroma. Clusters of tubular, mauve flowers appear on the plant during midsummer. Attractive to bees. It likes dry, well-drained soil.

6–12in / 16in

⬍ height and spread   ✳ feature of interest   ▮▮▮▮ season of interest   *TREES AND SHRUBS* **P – T**

AROMATIC CONIFERS

ABIES BALSAMEA ❷ 3–6
BALSAM FIR

PINACEAE

A slender, elegant conifer with dark green leaves, silvery-white on their undersides, that emit a strongly balsamlike fragrance when bruised. Oblong cones are produced later in the year. It is most often grown in one of its dwarf forms. It likes slightly acid, well-drained, but moisture-retentive soil.

CALOCEDRUS DECURRENS ❷ 5–8
INCENSE CEDAR

CUPRESSACEAE

Earlier known as *Libocedrus decurrens*, this distinctive, narrow, and upright conifer has glossy, bright green leaves in vertical fans. When bruised they emit a redolence reminiscent of incense and turpentine. The bark also emits this distinctive fragrance. Grow in a well-drained soil.

CHAMAECYPARIS LAWSONIANA ❷ 5–9
LAWSON'S CYPRESS

CUPRESSACEAE

A well-known conifer with small, dark green leaves that, when bruised, exude a fusion of parsley and resin. There are many varieties, some of them dwarf, with colored leaves which are ideal for planting in gardens. This conifer grows in any ordinary well-drained soil.

CHAMAECYPARIS OBTUSA ❷ 4–8
HINOKI CYPRESS

CUPRESSACEAE

A slow-growing conifer with bright green leaves which, when bruised, emit a distinctive warm and sweet redolence; it is said to resemble the aroma of pencils. There are several attractive forms for planting in gardens. It grows in any ordinary well-drained soil.

CHAMAECYPARIS PISIFERA ❷ 4–8
SAWARA CYPRESS

CUPRESSACEAE

Narrow and conical conifer with bright green, needlelike leaves borne in fernlike fans. When bruised they emit a fresh, resinlike scent. There are many forms that can be planted in gardens. It grows in any ordinary well-drained soil.

CHAMAECYPARIS THYOIDES ❷ 3–8
WHITE CYPRESS

CUPRESSACEAE

A slow-growing conifer with a conical habit and fans of glaucous bluish-green leaves. When bruised they have a warm and gingery redolence. It is most often seen in one of its small, garden-worthy forms. It grows in any ordinary moist soil.

🍃 leaf type　　　　　⬤ light preference　　　　　♌ speed of growth　　　　　❀ ease of growth

JUNIPERUS CHINENSIS ⓩ 3–9
CHINESE JUNIPER
CUPRESSACEAE

A popular conifer with dark green leaves that have a distinctive sour and resinous redolence. There are many attractive dwarf forms with colorful foliage, and they are ideal for planting in a garden. It thrives in any ordinary well-drained soil.

70ft / 20ft

JUNIPERUS COMMUNIS ⓩ 2–6
COMMON JUNIPER
CUPRESSACEAE

A conifer that forms either a small tree or a shrubby bush and bears prickly, light gray-green leaves with a single broad white band on the upper side. The foliage has an applelike scent when bruised. It thrives in any, preferably alkaline, well-drained soil.

1.5–20ft / 3–20ft

JUNIPERUS RECURVA ⓩ 7–10
DROOPING JUNIPER
CUPRESSACEAE

A distinctive conifer, ideal as a specimen tree in a large lawn, with pendulous branchlets bearing gray-green or green leaves. When bruised they have a paintlike bouquet, with a hint of turpentine. It thrives in any ordinary well drained soil.

30ft / 15ft

JUNIPERUS VIRGINIANA ⓩ 3–9
PENCIL CEDAR
CUPRESSACACEAE

A slow-growing tree with scalelike, pale to mid-green juvenile leaves. The adult leaves become pointed and finer. The foliage has the distinctive redolence of paint, with a hint of kitchen soap. It thrives in any ordinary well-drained soil.

50–100ft / 15–25ft

THUJA OCCIDENTALIS ⓩ 2–7
WHITE CEDAR
CUPRESSACEAE

A slow-growing conifer with flat, scalelike, dull green leaves, yellow beneath, that when bruised have an applelike scent, with a hint of incense. Several forms, some dwarf and with colorful foliage. It thrives in a moist, but well-drained soil.

30–60ft / 10–15ft

THUJA PLICATA ⓩ 6–8
WESTERN RED CEDAR
CUPRESSACEAE

A large, fast-growing conifer with scalelike, shiny mid-green leaves with undersides that reveal narrow white lines. When bruised, the leaves have an attractive pineapplelike fragrance. It thrives in a moist, but well-drained soil.

70–120ft / 20–30ft

⬍ height and spread   ✳ feature of interest   ▮▮▮ season of interest   *AROMATIC CONIFERS* **A – T**

WATER AND BOG GARDEN PLANTS

ACORUS CALAMUS 'VARIEGATUS' ● 4–11
SWEET FLAG
ARACEAE

A hardy, semiaquatic, rhizomatous-rooted herbaceous perennial with yellow and green, swordlike leaves with a camphorlike scent. The roots are similarly scented, while the yellow flowers have a tangerine scent with a hint of cinnamon. It is ideal for planting in water 3–5in (7.5–13cm) deep.

5ft / 24in

APONOGETON DISTACHYOS ● 9–10
WATER HAWTHORN
APONOGETONACEAE

A hardy, herbaceous, tuberous-rooted aquatic plant with narrowly oval, light-green leaves with maroon-brown markings. They float on the water's surface. From early summer to early autumn white, hawthorn-scented, deeply lobed flowers with black anthers appear on stems. Plant in water 9–18in (23–45cm) deep.

4in / 4ft

BUTOMUS UMBELLATUS ● 5–11
FLOWERING RUSH
BUTOMACEAE

A hardy, herbaceous perennial with rushlike green leaves that change to purple as they mature. During mid- and late summer it bears rose-pink flowers with a bitter, almondlike fragrance in umbrellalike heads on stems up to 4ft (1.2m) high. It is ideal for planting in bog gardens and in shallow water around ponds.

5ft / 18in

LYSICHITON AMERICANUS ● 7–9
YELLOW SKUNK CABBAGE
ARACEAE

A hardy herbaceous perennial with rich, golden-yellow, 9–18in (23–45cm) high, arumlike flowers from early to late spring. These are followed by large, leathery, grass-green colored leaves. It must be planted in moisture-retentive, fertile soil, in a bog garden or at the edge of a pond, and must not dry out in summer.

3ft / 4ft

NYMPHAEA 'FIRECREST' ● 4–11
WATER LILY
NYMPHAEACEAE

A hardy, aquatic perennial with rounded, deep green leaves and lightly scented pink flowers, 4–5in (10–13cm) wide, which change to deep pink and have red stamens. Blooming is throughout summer. It is ideal for planting in 6–18in (15–45cm) deep ponds. The leaves and flowers have a 2–4ft (60cm–1.2m) spread.

4ft

NYMPHAEA 'MARLIACEA ALBIDA' ● 4–11
WATER LILY
NYMPHAEACEAE

A hardy and very popular water lily with pure white, fragrant flowers throughout summer. Each is up to 6in (15cm) wide, with their backs flushed pale pink and with attractive yellow stamens. Plant it in water 1–2ft (30–60cm) deep. The leaves and flowers have a 4–5ft (1.2–1.5m) spread on the water's surface.

3–4ft

≋ leaf type   light preference   ⚥ speed of growth   ⚙ ease of growth

NYMPHAEA 'ODORATA SULPHUREA' ❷ 4–11
WATER LILY
NYMPHAEACEAE

A hardy water lily with rounded, glossy green leaves and lightly scented, canary-yellow, 6in (15cm) wide, star-shaped flowers with orange-yellow stamens. These appear all summer and tend to rise above the water's surface. Plant in water 6–18in (15–45cm) deep. The leaves and flowers have a 2–4ft (60cm–1.2m) spread.

3–4ft

NYMPHAEA 'W.B SHAW' ❷ 4–11
WATER LILY
NYMPHAEACEAE

A hardy and popular fragrant water lily which has soft pink, starlike flowers from mid- to late summer. Its leaves have a surface spread up to 3ft (90cm). Plant it in water 12–18in (30–45cm) deep.

3–4ft

PETASITES FRAGRANS ❷ 7–9
WINTER HELIOTROPE
ASTERACEAE

A rhizomatous-rooted perennial originally from the Mediterranean, this species has spoon-shaped toothed leaves. Between midwinter and early spring, it bears panicles of vanilla-scented lilac flower heads with a hint of almond. Grow in fertile, permanently moist soil and in a site in partial shade.

1ft
5ft

PRIMULA FLORINDAE ❷ 3–8
GIANT COWSLIP
PRIMULACEAE

A popular hardy border primula, ideal for planting alongside a pond or stream. It has large, oval, mid-green leaves and strong stems that bear drooping clusters of sweet, pale yellow flowers in early and midsummer. Grow in fertile, constantly moist soil.

4ft
3ft

PRIMULA SIKKIMENSIS ❷ 4–8
HIMALAYAN COWSLIP
PRIMULACEAE

A hardy border perennial with long, lance-shaped, pale green, and finely tooth-edged leaves. The funnel-shaped, pendent, sweetly scented, pale yellow, 3/4–1in (18–25mm) wide flowers are borne in clusters in early and midsummer. Grow in moderately fertile, constantly moist soil.

24–36in
24in

PRIMULA VIALII ❷ 5–8
PRIMROSE
PRIMULACEAE

A hardy and distinctive perennial primula with pale green, lance-shaped leaves covered in a white, powderlike dusting. The lightly scented, lavender-blue flowers are borne in dense, tapering spires during early and midsummer. Plant it in large, dominant drifts. Grow in moderately fertile, constantly moist soil.

12–24in
12in

⬍ height and spread   ✳ feature of interest   ▭▭▭ season of interest   *WATER AND BOG PLANTS* **A – P**

GLOSSARY

ALPINE: A plant that in its natural mountain habitat grows above the uppermost limit of trees. More colloquially, plants that are suitable for rock gardens are called alpines.

ANNUAL: A plant that grows from seed, flowers, and dies within the same year. Some half-hardy perennial plants are used as annuals; that is, they die off in the winter.

AQUATIC PLANT: A plant that lives totally or partly submerged in water.

BEDDING PLANTS: Plants that are set out for a temporary spring or summer display and discarded at the end of the season.

BIENNIAL: A plant raised from seed that makes its initial growth in one year and flowers during the following one, then dies.

BOG GARDEN PLANTS: Plants that live with their roots in moist soil.

BULB: An underground food storage organ formed of fleshy, modified leaves that enclose a dormant shoot.

CALYX: The outer and protective part of a flower. It is usually green and is very apparent in roses.

COMPOST: Vegetable waste from kitchens, as well as soft parts of garden plants, which is encouraged to decompose and to form a material that can be dug into soil or used to create a mulch around plants.

CORM: An underground storage organ formed of a swollen stem base, for example, a gladiolus.

CULTIVAR: A shortened term for "cultivated variety" that indicates a variety raised in cultivation. Strictly speaking, most modern varieties are cultivars, but the term variety is still widely used because it is familiar to most gardeners.

CUTTING: A section of plant which is detached and encouraged to form roots and stems to provide a new independent plant. Cuttings may be taken from roots, stems, or leaves.

DEADHEADING: The removal of a faded flower head to prevent the formation of seeds and to encourage the development of further flowers.

DECIDUOUS: Plants that lose their leaves during the winter are referred to as deciduous.

DORMANT: When a plant is alive but is making no growth, it is called dormant. The dormant period is usually the winter.

EVERGREEN: Plants that appear to be green throughout the year and not to lose their leaves are called evergreen. In reality, however, they shed some of their leaves throughout the year, while producing others.

FRIABLE: Soil that is crumbly, light, and easily worked. It especially applies to soil being prepared as a seedbed in spring.

HALF-HARDY: A plant that can withstand fairly low temperatures, but needs protection from frost.

HALF-HARDY ANNUAL: An annual that is sown in gentle warmth in a greenhouse in spring, the seedlings

being transferred to wider spacings in pots or boxes. The plants are placed in a garden or container only when all risk of frost has passed.

HARDEN OFF: To gradually accustom plants raised under cover to cooler conditions so that they can be planted outside.

HARDY: A plant that is able to survive outdoors in winter. In the case of some rock-garden plants, good drainage is essential to ensure their survival.

HERB: A plant that is grown for its aromatic qualities and can often be used in cooking or medicinally.

HERBACEOUS PERENNIAL: A plant with no woody tissue that lives for several years. It may be deciduous or evergreen.

HYBRID: A cross between two different species, varieties, or genera of plants.

LOAM: Friable topsoil.

MARGINAL PLANTS: Plants that live in shallow water at the edges of ponds. Some also thrive in boggy soil surrounding a pond.

MULCHING: Covering the soil around plants with well-decayed organic material such as garden compost, peat or, in the case of rock-garden plants, stone chippings or ¼ in (6mm) shingle.

NEUTRAL: Soil that is neither acid nor alkaline, with a pH of 7.0, is said to be neutral. Most plants grow in a pH of about 6.5.

PEAT: A naturally occurring substance formed from partly rotted organic material in water-logged soils, used as a growing medium and soil additive.

PERENNIAL: Any plant that lives for three or more years is called a perennial.

PERGOLA: An open timber structure made up of linked arches that is often covered with climbing plants.

POTTING SOIL: Traditionally, a soil formed of loam, sharp sand and peat, fertilizers, and lime. The ratio of the ingredients is altered according to the use that the soil will be put to, whther for sowing seeds, potting-up, or repotting plants into larger containers. Recognition of the environmental importance of conserving peat beds has led to many modern soils being formed of other organic materials, such as coir or shredded bark.

PRICKING OFF: Transplanting seedlings from the container in which they were sown to one where they are more widely spaced.

RACEME: An elongated flower head with each flower having a stem.

RAISED BED: A raised area, usually encircled by a drystone wall. Rock-garden plants can be grown both in the raised bed and the wall.

RHIZOME: An underground or partly buried horizontal stem. They can be slender or fleshy. Some irises have thick, fleshy rhizomes, while those of lily-of-the-valley are slender and creeping. They act as storage organs and perpetuate plants from one season to another.

ROSE TERMS: Several types of roses are featured in this book. They include: Alba (derived from *Rosa alba*, a species rose); Floribunda (sometimes known as Cluster Flowered Roses, with flowers borne in large clusters); Modern Shrub Rose (relatively recent hybrids, derived from Species and Old Roses); Hybrid Musk (a group of shrub roses derived from *Rosa moschata*); Polyantha Roses (small, bush-type roses which flower over a long period); New English Roses (shrub roses derived from Species and Old Roses).

SCREE BED: An area formed of small stones, together with a few large rocks, often positioned at the base of a rock garden.

SEED LEAVES: The first leaves that develop on a seedling, which are coarser and more robust than the true leaves.

SEMIEVERGREEN: A plant that may keep some of its leaves in a reasonably mild winter.

SPECIES ROSE: A term for a wild rose or one of its near relatives.

STAMEN: The male part of a flower, comprising the filament (stalk) and the anthers, which contain pollen.

STANDARD: A tree or shrub trained to form a rounded head of branches at the top of a clear stem.

STIGMA: The tip of the female part of a flower on which pollen alights.

SUBSHRUB: Small and spreading shrub with a woody base. It differs from normal shrubs in that, when grown in temperate regions, its upper stems and shoots die back during winter.

TILTH: Friable topsoil in which seeds are sown. It also acts as a mulch on the surface of soil, helping to reduce the loss of moisture from the soil's surface.

TOPSOIL: The uppermost fertile layer of soil that is suitable for plant growth.

TROUGH GARDENS: Old stone troughs partly filled with drainage material and then with freely draining compost. They are planted with miniature conifers and bulbs, as well as small rock-garden plants. These features are usually displayed on terraces and patios.

TUBER: A swollen, thickened and fleshy stem or root. Some tubers are swollen roots (dahlia), while others are swollen stems (potato). They serve as storage organs and help to perpetuate plants from one season to another.

VARIEGATED: Usually applied to leaves and used to describe a state of having two or more colors.

VARIETY: A naturally occurring variation of a species that retains its characteristics when propagated. The term is often used for cultivars.

WILDLIFE POND: An informal pond that encourages the presence of wildlife such as frogs, birds, insects, and small mammals.

INDEX

HARDINESS ZONES MAP

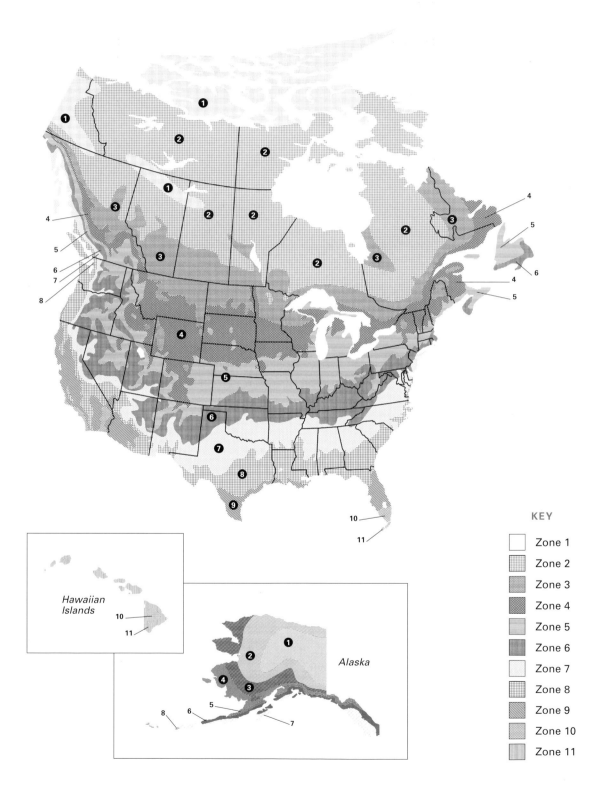

Hawaiian
Islands

Alaska

KEY

Zone 1
Zone 2
Zone 3
Zone 4
Zone 5
Zone 6
Zone 7
Zone 8
Zone 9
Zone 10
Zone 11